McCALL'S
Introduction to
ITALIAN
COOKING

McCALL'S
Introduction to
ITALIAN
COOKING

GALAHAD BOOKS · NEW YORK CITY

Library of Congress Catalog Card Number: 73-92824
ISBN 0-88365-199-8

Published by arrangement with Saturday Review Press,
division of E. P. Dutton & Co., Inc.

Printed in the United States of America

Contents

Illustrations follow pages 26, 42, 58 and 74

McCALL'S
Introduction to
ITALIAN
COOKING

Introduction

The cooking of Italy is regional, redolent of fresh herbs, employing the freshest of ingredients, reflecting the tastes and produce of the different geographic areas of the country. Each region—Venice, Genoa, Milan, Florence, Naples, Sicily—boasts of its specialties. Local products form the basis of each region's cuisine, so the dishes of Venice are not in the least like those of Naples, although both are seacoast cities. It follows that neighboring regions, perhaps no more than a few miles apart, but one on the coast, the other in the hills, will also eat quite different dishes.

Distinct as Italian cooking is in its regional variations, it has one thing in common—the universal freshness of the produce. It is not unusual even today for an Italian housewife to shop daily for fresh ingredients. The fruits, vegetables, meats, herbs, and cheeses are farm fresh, their flavor unimpaired by the processing and refrigerated storage that American food undergoes. A bowl of strawberries is fresh enough to perfume a room, bread is brought home still warm from the baker's, tomatoes are vine ripened, full of the savor of the sun, fruit stems are still decorated with bright green leaves.

Simplicity of preparation is also a hallmark of Italian cooking. To conserve fuel, most cooking is done on top of the stove, and baked goods are usually bought. Recipes make the most of seasonal foods, for they are both the least expensive and the most readily available.

Dishes are flavored with herbs—oregano, sweet basil, sage, parsley, rosemary—olives, wine, capers, anchovies, garlic, and cheese. Rice and butter form the basis of northern Italian cooking, while below Tuscany, in the south, olive oil and pasta are traditional and the flavor of the dishes is more pungent.

Milk-fed veal is the most common meat, and the most universally liked. Little beef is used, except in the central regions of the country, where it is good, for since Italy lacks pasturage, it is expensive to feed cattle to maturity. In the south, kid, or young goat, often replaces veal. Throughout Italy and especially in the south a variety of sausages is made, utilizing all possible parts of a butchered animal. Variety meats are used to flavor dishes of vegetables or starch. Fish and seafood, plentiful in the waters that surround the country, are also inexpensive and are consumed in quantity.

In Italian cookery, each dish is prepared with care and ingredients are combined with originality. An antipasto platter of cold meats and vegetables is arranged so that both the diner's eye and his palate are delighted; a simple slice of broiled veal is always garnished with slices of lemon and sprigs of parsley; the cook creates a lavish feast-day dessert with as much care as she arranges fresh fruit in a bowl.

Italian cuisine was the forerunner of French, for in the sixteenth century Florentine cooks introduced the art of cooking to the French court. However, Italian cooking has never placed the emphasis on rich sauces and elaborate garnishes that one finds in classic French cooking.

Regional Specialties

Seagirt Italy is suited to the development of regional dishes by both its geography and its history—the country was once split into numerous rival city-states. The Alps divide it from the rest of Europe, and the Apennine range down the length of the peninsula divides the country into hilly areas with a seacoast on either side. The branch of the Mediterranean known as the Tyrrhenian Sea borders Italy's long west coast. The Adriatic washes Italy's east coast, and at its head is Venice with her cuisine oriented toward seafood. A favorite Venetian dish is fritto misto di mare—scampi, squid, sole, and mullet dipped in flour, deep-fried, and served with parsley and lemon. Risi e bisi, rice and peas cooked in broth, is another traditional dish of the area, said to have been served at all official banquets of the old Republic of Venice. A fish stew of a dozen kinds of seafood called brodetto is also popular; across the peninsula, in Genoa, a very similar stew, full of octopus, squid, and cuttlefish, is known as burrida.

The north of Italy grows rice, the fine rice of the Piedmont, and corn meal, cooked into polenta, is also a staple starch. Risotto, rice cooked in stock or broth and flavored with butter, cheese, and bits of whatever is available, is a classic dish throughout the north. In Milan risotto is always flavored with saffron. Other dishes of Milan are osso buco, veal shanks; the thick, filling minestrone soup; peperonata or stewed sweet peppers, and mostarda di frutta, a relish of fruit in mustard sauce. In Turin, capital of the Piedmont, grissini, the slender bread sticks served with antipasti, are said to have originated. White truffles are a speciality of the region and flavor many dishes, including salads and fonduta, a fondue of Fontina, the native cheese. The north also produces one of the best blue cheeses, Gorgonzola, and another dessert cheese, Bel Paese.

On the western seacoast grow the lemons and oranges of the Italian Riviera, and the fresh basil that makes the famous pesto of Genoa, a sauce that is served with pasta or gnocchi or minestrone. In Bologna the sauce for noodles such as tagliatelle and the broader lasagne is ragu—vegetables and meat but without tomatoes. Pasta in the north is almost never dressed with tomato sauces, which are so widely used farther south.

Bologna produces mortadella, a sausage laced with pork fat that is designed for the antipasto course. From neighboring Parma come prosciutto, raw, cured ham that combines well with other meats or with fresh fruit, and the sharp grating cheese, Parmesan.

The extensive use of olive oil in cooking begins in central Italy, and in Umbria, spaghetti con aglio e olio (with garlic and oil) is popular. Florence lends her name to dishes made with spinach or garnished with it. Cakes are made with chestnut flour here. Another cake is the rich fruitcake, panforte, of Siena, and the macaroons of Perugia are famous as Christmas treats.

Tuscany is one of the few areas in Italy where beef is both good and cooked without a sauce, as in bistecca alla Fiorentina. Veal and pork chops are also broiled in this fashion. Chicken is flavored with olive oil and lemon juice. In Umbria pork is served as suckling pig and flavored with fennel. In neighboring Tuscany pork loin is roasted with chestnuts.

Farther south, in Rome, young lamb is roasted with garlic and rosemary, and thin slices of veal and ham combine in saltimbocca. Several famous Roman dishes use fettuccine, broad egg noodles. Rome's soup is stracciatella, chicken broth with beaten egg. Baby artichokes, only two inches in diameter and sometimes found in Italian markets in this country in the spring, are fried and are tender enough to eat whole. The cheese of the area is pecorino romano, a hard grating cheese similar to Parmesan.

Southern Italy, Naples, and the country throughout the boot and toe of the peninsula, is where the greatest varieties of pasta are eaten. Pasta is a staple, and is dressed with oil and garlic, clams, beans, and tomato sauces. Another favorite food of the south is pizza.

While lamb and kid are the usual meats, a great deal more fish is eaten every day. It is fried in olive oil, stewed in soups, or dried as in baccala (dried cod). Since meat is expensive, vegetables are relied upon. Eggplant is one of the most useful vegetables and combines well in dishes such as caponata, a vegetable antipasto.

The native cheeses of the south are the white, fresh mozzarella, which melts so well and is used to top pizza, and Provolone, which has a mild to sharp taste. Provolone is formed into many shapes and used in almost every course at table. Both cheeses were originally made of buffalo's milk, but today the cheese that is imported to this country is made of cow's milk.

Desserts in the south of Italy are varied and rich. Most of the country, except on feast days when an elaborate cake is bought from a bakery, finishes lunch and dinner with fresh fruit and cheese. Naples, however, often serves a tempting array of sweets, such as zuppa inglese, a trifle-like combination of spongecake and custard; gelato, ice cream; granita, fine ice crystals of lemon or coffee; coppa, a combination of the two; and the other frozen desserts, spumoni and tortoni.

The cooking of the island of Sicily is much like that of the southern mainland, for here, too, the land is poor. Pasta, tomatoes, vegetables, and the local sardines and tuna are the basis of most of the dishes. Ricotta, a favorite cheese in the south, sweetened and flavored with orange peel, is used to fill the pastry tubes of cannoli and alternates with spongecake layers in cassata alla Siciliana. Sardinia's dishes include songbirds flavored with wild myrtle, meat broth with dumplings, tuna, and saffron rice.

Dining as Italians Do

Breakfast in Italy is a light meal, as it is in France and Spain. It consists of caffè e latte, coffee with hot milk, or black coffee, a roll or a piece of white bread with jam. Lunch, generally served at one o'clock, is the big meal of the day; in the south it is followed by a siesta. Lunch begins with antipasto, which is followed either by a soup or a starch such as pasta, a rich dish, or gnocchi or polenta. This course, called asciutta or "dry soup," is most often served at lunch. The meat or fish course is accompanied by one or two vegetables or a salad. Fresh fruit, washed at the table in finger bowls and peeled and eaten with a knife and fork, and cheese end the meal. Black coffee is served after the fruit and cheese.

Dinner is usually served at seven-thirty and is similar to but lighter than lunch. Dinner begins with a cup of soup. The meat course may be accompanied by potatoes, and there will be vegetables and perhaps a salad. Meat is always carved in the kitchen and arranged on a platter with the vegetables and potato, and is then passed around the dining table.

The meal ends with fruit; if it is a formal dinner or festive occasion, a cake or dessert is served before the fruit.

White bread, fresh and soft inside with a good crust, is served at all three meals, but never with butter, unless buttered bread is suitable for the antipasto course. Bread is never served with pasta as it is so frequently in this country.

Wine is drunk at both lunch and dinner, and both meals invariably end with demitasse. Caffè espresso, served with a twist of lemon peel and sugar, and available at espresso bars or cafes, is drunk all day long.

Special Italian Ingredients

A number of foods are now imported from Italy, and these canned and bottled products are worth investing in, for they help to give Italian dishes their distinctive flavor.

All the ingredients mentioned in this book can be found either in gourmet food shops or in delicatessens, and many supermarkets now carry an excellent variety of Italian specialties.

One of the most important things in Italian cooking is to buy the finest quality olive oil you can afford. The best, most delicate oil is clear and light with a lovely green tinge. It is wise to buy small cans or bottles unless the oil will be used in quantity, for it turns rancid if it stands open in the kitchen cupboard. Always plug the pouring puncture in the can with waxed paper and keep the can in the refrigerator.

When fresh tomatoes are inexpensive, use them for tomato sauces, but the canned Italian plum tomatoes are an acceptable substitute. Some brands are already flavored with basil, as are the tomato pastes and purées that add concentrated flavor and color to sauces and main dishes. Fresh artichoke hearts for antipasti and salads are not available here, but the canned ones are very good. These ready-to-use hearts are packed in oil or in brine (if using the latter, refresh them by draining off the brine and rinsing them under cold water). Frozen hearts are often tougher and must be cooked before using. Canned beans—berlotti or red kidney beans, cannellini or white kidney beans, ceci or garbanzo beans, and fava, broad beans—are also good in an antipasto selection. They, too, should be drained and rinsed before tossing with an oil, vinegar, and herb dressing. Dried mushrooms are widely used in Italy for sauces and are a good addition to a dish when fresh mushrooms are not in season.

Anchovy fillets in oil are used in sauces, for antipasti, in pizza and salads. The variety that is rolled around a caper is particularly decorative. The finest tuna fish is imported from Italy, but American chunk style is also excellent for salads, antipasti, and sauces.

There is no real substitute for Italian prosciutto, but Canadian bacon is a better choice than boiled or baked ham slices. There are a number of Italian sausages that are served cold for antipasti: bologna, mild cured beef and pork; cappicola, pork seasoned with pepper; mortadella, pork and beef laced with cubes of fat; and the highly seasoned salami (cotto, campagnole, Genova, Milano, and the Sicilian varities, calamese and iola). All these sausages should be served thinly sliced.

Other useful imported foods are olives, both black and green, which are much more flavorful than the bland California variety, and capers in brine, good for garnishes and in salads.

Fresh herbs are an important part of Italian cooking, and are hard to find unless you can grow them. Parsley, which likes a cool temperature, makes a handsome pot plant on the kitchen window sill; choose the more pungent, flattish leafed, Italian type. Basil, used by the handful in Italy, is very easy to start from seed, or young plants can be bought in the spring in the Italian sections of large cities. Rosemary is best started from a cutting, and is invaluable for seasoning veal, lamb, and pork. Oregano, one of the most popular Italian herbs, gives pizza and many of the tomato sauces their special "Italian" taste. It is a hardy plant that needs sun and well-drained, fairly good soil; like rosemary it should be started from a cutting. Sage grows as a weed in Italy and can be easily started from seed.

For desserts, the flavor of pine nuts (also known as Indian nuts, pinons, and pignolas) is unique; they are carried in all health-food stores. Chestnuts are available in their shells in the winter, or canned or in sugar syrup.

Italian Cheeses

Cheese plays an important part in Italian cooking; there are many dozens of varieties in many sizes and shapes and textures. A number of them are eaten only locally, as is the case with much of the wine, which is only drunk in the region in which it is produced.

For truly authentic flavor in your Italian dishes, always use Italian cheeses. Never substitute, for instance, Cheddar for Parmesan or Muenster for mozzarella. When using a grating cheese like Parmesan, buy it in wedges and grate it as it is needed. It will be less expensive this way, and the flavor and texture of freshly grated cheese are incomparable.

Cheese should always be stored in the refrigerator. Soft cheeses, like Ricotta and mozzarella, should be used within a few days, but the harder cheeses—Provolone, cacciocavallo, Parmesan—can be kept for weeks. When serving cheese as an appetizer or for dessert, allow it to come to room temperature. An hour or two out of the refrigerator is all that is necessary.

Bel Paese: This semi-soft, creamy colored cheese is made from cow's milk. The flavor is mild to robust, and it is served in an antipasto selection and for dessert. In cooking it can be used in place of mozzarella.

Cacciocavallo: A firm cow's milk cheese from the south that is similar to Provolone but is not smoked. It is used for cooking and is eaten with fruit.

Fontina: A rich, semi-soft, whitish cheese of cow's or goat's milk. It melts well and can be eaten uncooked also.

Gorgonzola: Made of cow's milk or a combination of cow's and goat's milk, this is a superb, creamy, vein-mold cheese. The flavor is tangy, and it is served with fruit, as is the French Roquefort.

Mozzarella: Originally made of buffalo milk, it is usually made of cow's milk now. It is creamy white, firm, and elastic in consistency, and melts readily when heated.

Parmesan (Parmigiano-Reggiano): A very hard, ripened cheese of whole cow's milk, pale yellow in color with a rough, grainy texture. It is the finest grating cheese.

Provolone: A firm cow's milk cheese with a light interior and a brown or golden exterior. It is suitable for eating and, when aged, for cooking. It is pear- or sausage-shaped and is often seen hanging up, so that the air can pass freely around it. Flavor is mellow to sharp, and it is often smoked. Smaller sizes are provolette and provoloncini.

Ricotta: A soft, fresh cheese, white and moist, from the whey of cow's or sheep's milk. It must be absolutely fresh, and is frequently used with pasta, and in desserts.

Romano (also pecorino romano and sardo romano): A very hard grating cheese of cow's or sheep's milk, similar to Parmesan but with a sharper flavor. It is used in place of Parmesan in the south of Italy.

Stracchino: A soft, rich, eating cheese of cow's milk with a pungent flavor, which comes from Lombardy. Accompanied by a robust red wine, it is a good addition to the cheese tray.

Taleggio: A mild, soft, rich, and pale cheese of cow's milk, suitable as an appetizer and for dessert with fruit.

Italian Wines

Terraces of vines can be seen everywhere in Italy, reaching up the foothills of the Alps, bordering the northern lakes, down the length of the country to the sun-baked vineyards of the south and Sicily. Every province produces its own wine, a perfect accompaniment to the local food. Italy is one of the largest wine-growing countries in the world, largely exporting medium-quality and medium-price wines. Much of the country's wine is consumed at home, especially the yield of small vineyards.

The warm climate and fairly constant sunshine mean that vintage is not as significant in choosing Italian wines as it is for French and German, nor is the location of the vineyard important. Italian wines are young, light, and fresh; they are always a pleasure to drink.

Italian wines are known by the province where they are grown or by the variety of grape. The Piedmont produces some of the country's best wines. Among them are the red wines Barolo, perhaps Italy's greatest red, and Barbaresco, similar but less robust, and Italy's champagne, Asti Spumante. In Lombardy, good wines come from the Lake Garda vineyards and from the Valtellina mountainsides. Venice and Verona have excellent wines: Bardolino, a lively young red wine, Valpolicella, a smooth red wine, and Soave, one of the best white wines. Lambrusco, a slightly sparkling, dry red, is the wine of Bologna. Tuscany produces Chianti, Italy's best known red wine. Genuine Chianti has a black rooster on the seal of the bottle, and the better quality comes in bottles rather than in straw-covered fiaschi, or flagons.

Below Tuscany, Orvieto, a delicious and famous white wine that is both dry and semi-dry, and the somewhat similar Est! Est!! Est!!! are produced. Near Rome, Frascati, a dry white wine, is bottled. The wines of Naples are the red Falerno and Gragnano, and Lachrimae Christi, a white wine that is both dry and sweet. Sicily produces the sweet white Moscato wines and Marsala, a fortified wine that is drunk with desserts and used in cooking.

Red Italian wines should be served at "room" temperature or 55° to 65°F. The wine will probably be the right temperature if it has been stored in a closet, away from heating units. White wine should be chilled, but no more than an hour or two on the lower shelf of the refrigerator. Red wine goblets or tulip-shaped glasses are suitable for all Italian wines.

A dry white wine or a light red wine is drunk with the antipasto course. However, the flavor of wine cannot compete with marinated foods such as vegetable salads with vinegar in the dressing or with asparagus and artichokes, so it is preferable not to serve wine with these first courses.

For the rice or pasta course, the more delicate dishes like meatless risotti and fettuccine go well with dry white wine. Serve a light red wine with pasta that has a meat or tomato sauce. A rough red wine, a "country" wine, or vino da tavola, goes with pizza.

Fish is usually best complemented by a dry white wine, but a light red or rosé is more interesting with fried fish and fish stews and soups. Chicken and turkey are good with a light red wine, as are broiled, fried, and sautéed meats; beef and strongly flavored meat dishes take a full-bodied red wine.

At the end of the meal, a dry white wine is drunk with the mild cheeses; the more robust cheeses with a light red wine; and Gorgonzola needs a full-bodied red. The many sweet white wines are pleasant with desserts, and any of the semi-sweet or sweet sparkling white wines would be perfect at the end of a dinner party. Unless the meal is a special occasion or a formal dinner, it is customary in Italy to serve only one type of wine.

WHITE WINES

Dry: Capri Blanco, Cortese, Est! Est!! Est!!!, Falerno, Frascati, Lachrimae Christi, Orvieto, Sansevero, Soave, Terlano, Valtellina.
Semi-Dry and Semi-Sweet: Albana di Romagna, Coronata, Dolcevere, Est! Est!! Est!!!, Frascati, Orvieto Termeno Aromatico, Verdicchio di Fesi.
Sparkling: Asti Spumante, Prosecco, Bianco di Scandiano.
Sweet: Aleatico di Puglia, Malvasia, Marsala, Moscato, Vino Santo.

RED WINES

Light: Bardolino, Chianti, Freisa, Grignolino, Grumello, Lambrusco, Nebbiolo, Rosso Piceno, Sangue di Giuda, Valtellina (Sassella).

Full-Bodied: Barbaresco, Barbera, Barolo, Falerno, Gattinara, Inferno, Santa Maddalena, Valpolicella.

APERITIFS

Sweet red and white vermouth and dry white vermouth: Campari, Punto e Mes.

LIQUEURS

Centerbe (herb flavored), Galliano (herbs), Genepi (gentian flowers). Kapriol (bitter herbs), Maraschino (cherries), Mistra and Sambuca (anise), Strega (herbs).

Giving an Italian Party

Italians love to entertain, and often even family dinners assume a party air. Giving an Italian party, once you have mastered a group of recipes,° is a pleasure, for much of the preparation can be done ahead, leaving the hostess-cook time to enjoy her guests. The food should always be attractively arranged and presented, whether it is for a formal dinner with your best china, linen, and silver, a cocktail party, or a pizza party.

A formal Italian dinner party is always served in the dining room with a magnificently set table—the family's heirloom china and silver, damask cloth, and lace-edged napkins. Italians usually do not have flowers on the table, but a centerpiece of white, red, and black grapes in a crystal or silver bowl would be both handsome and suitable.

Begin dinner by serving aperitifs in the living room. White or red vermouths and Campari with soda are typical drinks; Italians rightly feel that mixed drinks and liquor dull the palate for the elaborate dinner to follow. For the same reason, no antipasti are served with the drinks, although bowls of black and green olives could be placed around the room. One or at the most two drinks are consumed before going into the dining room.

The meal itself begins with an antipasto of Melon Balls Prosciutto. The next course could be either soup, Stracciatella, or a simple fillet of sole, fried in oil and butter, garnished with lemon wedges and parsley sprigs. A glass of white wine, Soave or dry Orvieto, should accompany the fish. The meat is Italian Pork Chops Marsala and is accompanied by zucchini, thinly sliced and sautéed with butter and basil until just barely done.

° *Recipes for all the dishes in this section are in the book.*

A light red wine like Bardolino is a good choice with the meat course. Although the fish must be cooked just before serving, both the pork chops and zucchini can be prepared ahead.

The salad, Green Salad, should be served as a separate course. The dessert can be Spumoni or an elegant Chocolate and Coffee Ice Cream Bombe, or cold Zabaglione with fresh strawberries. The dinner party ends with espresso, served in demitasse cups with twists of lemon peel and Torrone (Nougat).

A summer family reunion or festive dinner, eaten at two o'clock Sunday afternoon, could be served either in the dining room, if it is big enough, or set out buffet style on a shaded terrace. Fill decanters with Chianti and place them on small tables set for four or six, and then let everyone help himself to the food. Except for the dessert and coffee, the food should be arranged on a long table with plates, silver and large, bright cloth napkins (don't use paper napkins, for they tend to blow away). Decorate the table with baskets of fresh fruit in season and baskets of freshly sliced Italian bread and grissini, and butter curls in bowls of cracked ice.

Arrange two or three antipasto platters of thinly sliced sausages, roasted red and green peppers, quartered hard-cooked eggs, black and green olives, radish roses, cherry tomatoes with their stems, and salads of marinated green beans, chick-peas, and red kidney beans, served in small lettuce-leaf cups. A hot dish, Baked Lasagne or Baked Ziti Casserole, should be on the table with a cold one like Cold Veal with Tuna Fish Sauce. Both dishes can be prepared the day before. No vegetables or potatoes are necessary.

Dessert should be lavish. The fresh fruit of the table decorations should be eaten with cheese—Bel Paese, Provolone, stracchino, and Fontina— and bread while the last of the wine is drunk. Then clear the buffet table and bring out the coffee service and luscious Sicilian Cream Cake or an ice cream dessert like Della Robbia Ice Cream Wreath. Pass plates of little cookies—Amaretti, Pinocatte, and Regina—with the coffee. A hostess can expect a party like this to last three or four hours at the table.

A teen-age party should feature pizza. Have it in the recreation room or on the terrace where the teen-agers can dance to Italian records. Cola and fruit-flavored soft drinks are immensely popular in Italy and are perfect for this type of Saturday night get-together. Serve it buffet style with antipasto platters or several vegetable salads. Artichoke-Tomato Salad with Fresh Herb Dressing or Green Bean and Potato Salad. Make individual Home-style Pizza pies and plan on two 8- or 9-inch-diameter pizzas for each guest. Place anchovy fillets, sautéed mushrooms, sliced pepperoni sausage, roasted green and red peppers, tiny meatballs, slices of mozzarella and extra grated Parmesan cheese in bowls on the table so the teen-agers can decorate their own pizzas before they are popped into the oven. Dessert should be a bowl of scoops of six or eight different ice creams—peach, chocolate, vanilla, and coffee, etc.—and Cenci, piled high on a plate and dusted with confectioners' sugar.

One of the most successful parties to give is an American cocktail-buffet with Italian food and ambiance. The room should be decorated with Italian colors—red, green, and white. These colors should appear in the bowls of flowers and leaves set around the room; on the bar table the paper napkins should be red and green, and the buffet table should be covered with a white cloth so that the plates and the napkins can be red and green. Use paper, enamel, plastic, or china plates and cloth or paper napkins. If you have any dishes in that charming and colorful Italian peasant pottery, use them by all means. Make sure there is a good selection of Italian records—film scores and Italian popular singers—for the phonograph.

Besides the usual selection of highballs and cocktails, serve Italian vermouth over ice cubes with a twist of lemon peel, and red wine (Chianti or Valpolicella) and white wine (dry Frascati or Soave). The wine is to be drunk as the party begins by those who want it and by everyone with the buffet supper.

The food should begin with bowls of olives, garlic-flavored and plain, and several platters of small cold antipasti: marinated artichoke hearts; anchovy-stuffed eggs, quartered; cherry tomatoes; cubes of Bel Paese, Provolone, and mozzarella; cubes of several kinds of salamis; rolled slices of prosciutto and mortadella; radish roses; strips of fennel; and celery hearts. These should be arranged as artistically as possible in rows and circles on lettuce-covered platters, and should be passed around. Have bowls of sesame-seed-covered grissini within reach. Large platters of hot Stuffed Clams Oregano, made the day before and served with little wooden forks, should be passed after the antipasto platters have been around two or three times. Make four to six stuffed clams per guest.

If the party begins at six o'clock, plan to serve the buffet between eight and nine-thirty, depending on how hungry the guests seem. As the food is brought out to the buffet table, clear the bar of everything but the red and white wines and glasses for the wine.

There should be several main dishes that can be prepared ahead and reheated, and a green salad. Good choices for hot dishes are Shrimp Lasagne, Homemade Ravioli, Baked Manicotti, or Italian Rice and Sausage. Choose two of these dishes, or one and a platter of hot, stuffed, individual eggplants and zucchini or a casserole of Eggplant Parmesan. Also have a meat dish that can be easily eaten with a fork: Cold Veal with Tuna Fish Sauce, especially good for summer parties, or Uova in Umido alla Fiorentina, colorful egg and veal rolls which are served at room temperature. The best salad is a large crystal bowl of several kinds of lettuce, watercress, rugula (a sharp Italian green), and chicory, simply dressed with oil and vinegar and a touch of garlic.

Dessert should be simple and should herald the end of the party. It should be nothing more than plates of cookies—Regina and Amaretti—passed with cups of espresso.

Appetizers & Salads

APPETIZERS
Antipasti

Antipasto means "before the meal" and is the first course of the day's main meal. A selection of antipasti or a substantial salad with meat and vegetables can also be the light meal of the day. It is eaten with white bread, occasionally served with butter, and wine, cheese, and fruit. An antipasto can be simple, a few garlic-flavored olives, tomato slices, and a slice or two of mortadella and salami; or elaborate, a beautifully arranged platter of eight or ten different salads and meats; or elegant, prosciutto with melon. A light antipasto, for example, one of the vegetable salads, should precede a substantial or highly seasoned meat course; a main course of broiled fish or chicken can begin with a complete antipasto platter.

The typical Italian antipasto is a selection of cold foods either prepared at home or bought at the salumeria, or delicatessen. The portions of meats, vegetables, and salads should be kept small, since the purpose of the antipasto is to whet the appetite, not surfeit it. A hot antipasto is good in the winter, and the stuffed vegetables in Chapter 6 make delicious first courses. An attractive combination is small stuffed eggplants, zucchini, and tomatoes. The stuffings may be the same for each vegetable, or bits of salami can be added to the zucchini; chopped clams or sautéed ground beef to the eggplant; and chopped anchovy fillets to the tomato.

Antipasto Platter

PIATTO DI ANTIPASTI

This is a quick and colorful version of the classic antipasto platter. Serve it with crusty Italian bread and sweet butter curls.

Dressing
1 bottle (8 ounces) oil-and-vinegar dressing
2 tablespoons pickle relish
1 tablespoon lemon juice
½ teaspoon Worcestershire sauce

1 can (1 pound) whole green beans
1 can (1 pound) tiny whole carrots

1 can (1 pound, 4 ounces) chick-peas
1 can (3½ ounces) tiny green peas
1 can (1 pound) sliced pickled beets
1 can (9¼ ounces) chunk-style tuna

Crisp lettuce leaves

1. Make Dressing: In small bowl, combine oil-and-vinegar dressing, pickle relish, lemon juice, and Worcestershire.

2. Drain green beans, carrots, chick-peas, and green peas. Arrange in separate groups in a shallow dish. Pour dressing over all.

3. Refrigerate, covered, until very well chilled—several hours or overnight. Also refrigerate beets and tuna.

4. To serve: Place lettuce on round platter. Arrange tuna in center; surround with vegetables.

Makes 8 servings.

Pickled Garden Relish

VERDURE MARINATE

½ small head cauliflower, cut in flowerets and sliced
2 carrots, pared, cut in 2-inch strips
2 stalks celery, cut in 1-inch pieces (1 cup)
1 green pepper, cut in 2-inch strips
1 jar (4 ounces) pimiento, drained, cut in strips

1 jar (3 ounces) pitted green olives, drained
¾ cup wine vinegar
½ cup olive or salad oil
2 tablespoons sugar
1 teaspoon salt
½ teaspoon dried oregano leaves
¼ teaspoon pepper

1. In large skillet, combine ingredients with ¼ cup water. Bring to boil; stir occasionally. Reduce heat; simmer, covered, 5 minutes.

2. Cool; then refrigerate at least 24 hours.
3. Drain well.
Makes 6 servings.

The next five recipes are all suitable for the antipasto platter, and a happy combination would be artichoke hearts, roasted peppers, and stuffed eggs, decorated with garlic olives and radish roses and arranged on a bed of curly endive.

Anchovy-stuffed Eggs

UOVA CON ACCIUGHE

6 hard-cooked eggs	2 teaspoons lemon juice
6 flat anchovies, drained and chopped	Dash pepper
	2 tablespoons chopped parsley
3 tablespoons mayonnaise or cooked salad dressing	1 pimiento, drained
	Bottled capers, drained

1. Cut eggs in half lengthwise. Remove yolks to a small bowl. Add anchovies, mayonnaise, lemon juice, pepper, and parsley; mix well with fork.
2. Stuff egg whites with yolk mixture, mounding it with fork.
3. Cut pimiento into 24 strips 1 inch long.
4. Arrange 2 strips crisscross on each egg half. Garnish with 2 capers, one at each end.
Makes 12.

Garlic Olives

OLIVE ALL'AGLIO

1 can (7 ounces) large pitted ripe olives, undrained	¼ teaspoon crushed red pepper
½ cup red-wine vinegar	1 clove garlic, minced
¼ cup olive oil	¼ cup finely chopped onion
	1 teaspoon dried oregano leaves

1. Turn olives and their liquid into a quart jar with tight-fitting lid.
2. Add vinegar and rest of ingredients; cover tightly; shake well.
3. Refrigerate several days, shaking jar occasionally. Drain just before serving.
Makes about 36.

Marinated Artichoke Hearts

CARCIOFI MARINATI

2 packages (9-ounce size) frozen artichoke hearts	1 clove garlic, crushed
1 teaspoon salt	1 tablespoon finely chopped parsley
	1 tablespoon finely chopped onion
Marinade	½ teaspoon dried oregano leaves
¼ cup lemon juice	½ teaspoon salt
¼ cup olive oil	Dash pepper
¼ cup red-wine vinegar	

1. Cook artichoke hearts as package label directs, using the salt and amount of water specified on package. Drain; cool slightly.

2. Make Marinade: In jar with tight-fitting lid, combine all marinade ingredients; shake vigorously to combine well.

3. Pour marinade over artichokes in large bowl; toss to coat artichokes well.

4. Refrigerate, covered, 4 hours, stirring occasionally.

Makes 6 servings.

Roasted Peppers

PEPERONI ALLA PIEMONTESE

8 medium sweet red peppers (2½ pounds)	2 teaspoons salt
1 cup olive oil	3 small cloves garlic
¼ cup lemon juice	3 anchovy fillets

1. Preheat oven to 450°F.

2. Wash red peppers, and drain them well.

3. Place peppers on cookie sheet; bake about 20 minutes, or until the skin of the peppers becomes blistered and charred. Turn the peppers every 5 minutes with tongs.

4. Place hot peppers in a large kettle; cover kettle and let peppers stand 15 minutes.

5. Peel off charred skin with sharp knife. Cut each pepper into fourths. Remove the ribs and seeds and cut out any dark spots.

6. In large bowl, combine olive oil, lemon juice, salt, and garlic. Add the peppers, and toss lightly to coat with oil mixture.

7. Pack pepper mixture and anchovy fillets into a 1-quart jar; cap. Refrigerate several hours or overnight. Serve as an appetizer, or use in a tossed salad.

Makes 1 quart.

Marinated Tomato Slices

POMODORI MARINATI

4 large tomatoes	½ teaspoon minced garlic
	½ teaspoon salt
Marinade	½ teaspoon oregano leaves
¼ cup olive oil	
1 tablespoon lemon juice	

1. Peel and slice tomatoes. Arrange in a shallow dish.
2. Combine the marinade ingredients and pour over the tomatoes.
3. Refrigerate, covered, 1 hour.

Makes 6 servings.

Eggplant Appetizer

CAPONATA

1 large eggplant (1½ pounds)	2 tablespoons sugar
½ cup plus 2 tablespoons olive oil	2 tablespoons drained capers
2½ cups sliced onion	½ teaspoon salt
1 cup diced celery	Dash pepper
2 cans (8-ounce size) tomato sauce	12 pitted ripe olives, cut in slivers
¼ cup red-wine vinegar	Toast rounds

1. Wash eggplant; cut into ½-inch cubes.
2. In ½ cup hot oil in large skillet, sauté eggplant until tender and golden brown. Remove eggplant, and set aside.
3. In 2 tablespoons hot oil in same skillet, sauté onion and celery until tender—about 5 minutes.
4. Return eggplant to skillet. Stir in tomato sauce; bring to boiling. Reduce heat, and simmer, covered, 15 minutes.
5. Add vinegar, sugar, capers, salt, pepper, and olives. Simmer, covered, and stirring occasionally, 20 minutes longer.
6. Refrigerate eggplant mixture, covered, overnight.

7. To serve: Turn mixture into serving bowl. Surround with toast rounds.

Makes 6 to 8 servings.

Melon Balls Prosciutto

ANTIPASTO DI MELONE E PROSCIUTTO

In season Persian or Cranshaw melon or a large cantaloupe can be substituted for the honeydew. In Italy fresh green or black figs are also served with prosciutto in the summer.

¼ pound thinly sliced prosciutto	1 (2½-pound) honeydew melon

1. Cut prosciutto into strips 2 inches long and ½ inch wide.

2. With sharp knife, cut a zigzag line around middle of melon, cutting through to center.

3. Pull melon halves apart; scoop out seeds and fibers. Trim a slice from bottom of one of the halves to make it stand level; reserve.

4. With melon-ball cutter, scoop out enough balls to measure 3 cups.

5. Wrap each ball in a strip of prosciutto; secure with wooden pick.

6. Mound balls into reserved melon half; cover with plastic film. Refrigerate 1 hour, or until ready to use.

Makes 8 servings.

Stuffed Clams Oregano

VONGOLE RIPIENE ALL'OREGANO

Flavored with Italy's favorite herb, stuffed clams are one of the best of the hot appetizers. Canned chopped clams (2 cans, 7-ounce size) may be used if fresh ones are not available; scallop shells or small baking dishes can be substituted for the clamshells.

2 dozen clams in shells, well scrubbed	4 teaspoons lemon juice
¾ cup butter or margarine, melted	1 teaspoon dried oregano leaves
1 cup packaged dry bread crumbs	⅛ teaspoon liquid hot-pepper seasoning
2 cloves garlic, crushed	Rock salt
2 tablespoons chopped parsley	Lemon wedges
2 tablespoons grated Parmesan cheese	Parsley sprigs

1. In large kettle, bring ½ inch water to boiling. Add clams; simmer, covered, until clams open—6 to 10 minutes.

2. Meanwhile, in medium bowl, combine butter with bread crumbs, garlic, chopped parsley, Parmesan, lemon juice, oregano, and hot-pepper seasoning.

3. Remove the clams from kettle; discard top shells. Remove clams from bottom shells; chop coarsely, and add to crumb mixture. Spoon into bottom shells.

4. Place a layer of rock salt, ½ inch deep, in a large roasting pan or two shallow casseroles; sprinkle with water to dampen.

5. Arrange filled clamshells on salt. Run under broiler just until golden brown—about 5 minutes. Garnish with lemon wedges and parsley sprigs. Serve at once.

Makes 8 servings.

Green and White Asparagus Vinaigrette

ASPARAGI MARINATI

2 packages (10-ounce size) frozen jumbo green-asparagus spears	¼ teaspoon salt
	⅛ teaspoon pepper
½ cup olive oil	2 cans (15-ounce size) white-asparagus spears, drained
½ cup vinegar	1 can (7-ounces) pitted ripe olives, drained
2 teaspoons sugar	
½ teaspoon dried basil leaves	Crisp lettuce
½ teaspoon dry mustard	

1. Cook asparagus as package label directs; drain well.

2. Combine oil, vinegar, sugar, basil, dry mustard, salt, and pepper in jar with tight-fitting lid; shake vigorously to blend.

3. In 13-by-9-by-2-inch glass baking dish, place cooked green asparagus, white asparagus, and olives. Add oil-and-vinegar mixture.

4. Refrigerate, covered, 4 to 6 hours. Carefully turn asparagus spears once or twice.

5. To serve: With slotted utensil, remove asparagus and olives from dressing; arrange on bed of lettuce.

Makes 12 servings.

PIZZA

Naples is the home of pizza, which at first was a workingman's dish. Today pizzerias, small restaurants where pizza is baked to order, are popular
in all the big cities. Pizza is a thin circle of yeast bread dough, smothered
with tomato sauce flavored with oregano and cheese, and decorated with
combinations of anchovies, onions, sausage, mushrooms, peppers, and
black olives, or whatever your appetite suggests. It is baked on a large,
flat pizza tray.

Pizza is eaten at all hours in Italy, and plate-sized pizza is a supper
dish, while individual pizzette, 6 inches in diameter, are served as antipasto.

These are typical pizza recipes, adapted for American kitchens. Eat
pizza hot and straight from the oven, for the dough toughens quickly.

Home-style Pizza with Tomatoes and Olives

PIZZA ALLA CASALINGA

1½ packages (9½-ounce size) piecrust mix	¾ teaspoon salt
	¾ teaspoon dried oregano leaves
8 large ripe tomatoes (4 pounds)	4 cups thinly sliced onion
	½ cup grated Parmesan cheese
6 tablespoons butter or margarine	2 cans (2-ounce size) anchovy fillets, drained
2 cloves garlic, crushed	½ cup pitted ripe olives, sliced

1. Prepare piecrust mix as package label directs. Shape into a ball;
divide in half. On lightly floured surface, roll out half to a 13-inch circle.
Use to line a 12-inch pizza pan. Prick well with fork. Refrigerate until
ready to use. Repeat with other half.

2. Peel the tomatoes; cut each into thick slices and remove seeds. Set
aside.

3. In 3 tablespoons butter in large skillet, sauté garlic until golden. Add
tomato, salt, and oregano, crushing tomato with potato masher; bring to
boiling. Reduce heat, and simmer, stirring occasionally, 45 minutes, or
until mixture is thick.

4. Preheat oven to 450°F. Bake crusts 10 minutes.

5. Meanwhile, in 3 tablespoons hot butter in large skillet, sauté onion until golden and tender—about 10 minutes.

6. Sprinkle cheese over crusts; top with onion, then with tomato mixture. Arrange anchovy fillets and olive slices on tomato mixture.

7. Bake 25 to 30 minutes, or until bubbly and heated through. Makes 16 servings.

Sausage Pizza

PIZZA DI SALSICCE

1 package (13¼ ounces) frozen sausage pizza	6 pitted ripe olives, sliced
2 small tomatoes	2 slices mozzarella cheese
	½ cup shredded lettuce, crisped

1. Preheat oven to 450°F.

2. Remove pizza from package.

3. Slice tomatoes; cut slices in half. Arrange, slightly overlapping, around edge of pizza; lay olive slices inside tomato slices.

4. Cut cheese into strips; sprinkle over tomato.

5. Place directly on oven rack; bake 12 to 15 minutes, or until crust is golden and cheese bubbling.

6. To serve: Mound lettuce in center of pizza. Cut in wedges; serve immediately.

Makes 4 servings.

Note: You may wish to use 2 frozen pizzas, and double other ingredients, to make 8 servings.

SALADS

Insalate

Decorative salads of vegetables and fish (anchovy fillets, tuna in olive oil, or cold, cooked shellfish) make good antipasti. They should be followed by pasta with a meat sauce or a substantial meat dish. The Green Bean and Potato Salad is particularly nice before a lamb or veal recipe. The Artichoke-Tomato Salad and the Cauliflower Salad can be served as an antipasto or they can accompany the meat course. When served with the meat, these salads are so filling that another vegetable is not necessary.

Garbanzo Bean Salad

INSALATA DI CECI

An equally good Italian-style salad can be prepared by substituting canned red kidney beans or cooked lentils for the garbanzo beans.

2 cups diced potato
1 cup thinly sliced carrot
1 large red onion, thinly sliced
¼ cup olive oil
2 cans (1-pound size)
   garbanzo beans, drained

½ cup Italian-style dressing
2 cloves garlic, crushed
2 teaspoons salt
1½ teaspoons sugar

1. In large saucepan, in 1 inch salted boiling water, cook potato and carrot until tender—about 10 minutes. Drain; turn into large bowl.
2. In medium, heavy skillet, sauté onion in oil until soft but not brown. Add to potato and carrot.
3. Drain garbanzos. Add to potato mixture.
4. In small bowl, combine dressing, garlic, salt, and sugar; mix well. Pour over vegetable mixture.
5. Toss gently until well mixed. Serve warm. Or refrigerate 2 hours, or until well chilled.
   Makes 8 servings.

Green Bean and Potato Salad

INSALATA DI FAGIOLINI E PATATE

1 pound small new potatoes,
   well scrubbed
1 package (9 ounces) frozen
   Italian green beans

Cheese Dressing
¼ cup olive oil
¼ cup red-wine vinegar

2 tablespoons grated Parmesan
   cheese
1 teaspoon seasoned salt
½ teaspoon dried oregano leaves
⅛ teaspoon pepper

2 cups bite-size pieces escarole
Grated Parmesan cheese

1. Cook potatoes, covered, in boiling water just until tender—about 25 minutes.
2. Drain potatoes; cool. Peel, and cut into cubes.
3. Meanwhile, cook the Italian green beans as the package label directs; drain.
4. Make Cheese Dressing: In jar with tight-fitting cover, combine oil,

vinegar, 2 tablespoons grated cheese, the seasoned salt, oregano, and pepper. Shake to mix well.

5. In large bowl, combine potato, beans, and Cheese Dressing; toss lightly, to coat vegetables well. Refrigerate, covered, until very well chilled—at least 2 hours.

6. Just before serving, toss escarole with potato and beans. Generously sprinkle top with grated cheese.

Makes 6 servings.

Cauliflower Salad

INSALATA DI CAVOLFIORE

2 cups thinly sliced raw cauliflower	**Dressing**
½ cup chopped pitted ripe olives	4½ tablespoons olive oil
⅓ cup finely chopped green pepper	1½ tablespoons lemon juice
	1½ tablespoons wine vinegar
¼ cup chopped pimiento	1 teaspoon salt
3 tablespoons chopped onion	¼ teaspoon sugar
	Dash pepper

1. In medium bowl, combine cauliflower, olives, green pepper, pimiento, and onion.

2. Make Dressing: In small bowl, combine oil, lemon juice, vinegar, salt, sugar, and pepper; beat with rotary beater until well blended. Pour over cauliflower mixture.

3. Refrigerate, covered, until well chilled—at least 1 hour.

4. To serve: Spoon salad into bowl, or, if desired, arrange on lettuce on individual salad plates.

Makes 4 servings.

Artichoke-Tomato Salad with Fresh-Herb Dressing

INSALATA DI CARCIOFI E POMODORI

1 lemon, cut into eighths	**Fresh-Herb Dressing***
2 teaspoons salt	½ cup tarragon vinegar
3 large artichokes, or 2 packages (10-ounce size) frozen artichoke hearts	1 cup olive oil
	¼ cup chopped parsley
	2 tablespoons finely snipped chives

* *Or use 1½ cups bottled oil-and-vinegar dressing. If you make dressing, you may use ½ tablespoon dried tarragon leaves and ½ tablespoon dried basil leaves instead of fresh herbs.*

1 tablespoon chopped fresh tarragon leaves	⅛ teaspoon pepper
1 tablespoon chopped fresh basil leaves	4 tomatoes (about 2½ pounds)
1 teaspoon sugar	8 pitted ripe olives
1 teaspoon salt	Chicory

1. In 6-quart kettle, bring 3 quarts water, the lemon, and 2 teaspoons salt to boiling.

2. Meanwhile, wash artichokes. Trim stalks from bottoms; remove discolored and tough outer leaves. Cut 1 inch from tops; with scissors, snip off spiky ends of leaves. Cut into quarters; remove fuzzy chokes.

3. Drop into seasoned boiling water; return to boiling. Reduce heat; boil gently, covered, until bases of artichokes are tender—about 15 minutes. Drain well. If using frozen artichoke hearts, cook as package label directs.

4. Place, cut side up, in single layer in shallow dish.

5. Make Fresh-Herb Dressing: In pint jar with tight-fitting lid, combine vinegar, oil, parsley, chives, tarragon, basil, sugar, salt, and pepper; shake well.

6. Spoon about ⅔ of dressing over warm artichokes. Cover and refrigerate, basting occasionally with dressing, until very well chilled—at least 4 hours. Cover and refrigerate remaining dressing.

7. At serving time: Cut tomatoes into eighths; place in medium bowl. Add olives and reserved dressing; toss to mix.

8. Arrange artichokes around edge of large serving platter. Pile tomato mixture in center. Garnish with chicory.

Makes 6 to 8 servings.

Anchovy Salad

INSALATA DI ACCIUGHE

This makes a handsome and pungent antipasto. Fish or seafood salads should not accompany the meat dish. This salad would be best served as a separate course before a bland pasta or a steak or roast.

2 cans (2-ounce size) anchovy fillets, drained	1 tablespoon finely chopped onion
¼ cup diced pickled beets	1 tablespoon drained capers
2 tablespoons finely chopped green pepper	2 tablespoons olive oil
	4 teaspoons red-wine vinegar

½ teaspoon sugar
½ teaspoon dried oregano leaves
Dash pepper
Crisp chicory leaves

Hard-cooked egg wedges
Whole pickled beets
Drained capers

1. In bowl, combine anchovies, beets, green pepper, onion, and capers.
2. In jar with tight-fitting lid, combine oil, vinegar, sugar, oregano, pepper; shake vigorously. Pour over anchovy mixture and toss.
3. Refrigerate, covered, at least 2 hours.
4. To serve: Spoon on chicory on serving plate. Garnish with eggs, beets, capers. Pass chunks of Italian bread.
Makes 4 servings.

Green Salad

INSALATA MISTA

The next two salads of fresh greens and spinach with their simple dressings should be served with meat dishes. They are light enough so that potatoes and a hot vegetable can be included in the menu.

1 small head Boston lettuce
1 small head Bibb lettuce
½ small head romaine
1 Belgian endive
½ clove garlic

6 tablespoons olive oil
3 tablespoons tarragon vinegar
1 teaspoon salt
Freshly ground black pepper

1. Prepare salad greens: Wash lettuce, romaine, and endive, and separate into leaves, discarding discolored or bruised leaves. Drain well, shaking in salad basket or placing on paper towels to remove excess moisture.
2. Place cleaned greens in plastic bag, or wrap in plastic film. Refrigerate until crisp and cold—several hours. Also refrigerate salad bowl.
3. At serving time, rub inside of salad bowl with garlic; discard garlic. Tear greens in bite-size pieces into bowl; leave small leaves whole.
4. In jar with tight-fitting lid, combine oil, vinegar, salt, and dash pepper; shake until well combined.
5. Pour half of dressing over greens. With salad spoon and fork, toss greens until they are well coated and no dressing remains in bottom of bowl. Add more dressing, if desired.
Makes 6 to 8 servings.

Fresh Spinach Salad

INSALATA DI SPINACI

Dressing
2 tablespoons white-wine
  vinegar
2 tablespoons lemon juice
½ cup olive oil
1 teaspoon salt
¼ teaspoon pepper
1 teaspoon sugar
½ teaspoon dry mustard
1 clove garlic (optional)

Salad
¾ pound tender young spinach
6 green onions, thinly sliced
  (¼ cup)
½ cup sliced radishes
1 small cucumber, pared and
  thinly sliced

1. Make Dressing: Combine all dressing ingredients in jar with tight-fitting lid; shake vigorously. Refrigerate until ready to use.

2. Make Salad: Wash spinach, and remove stems. Tear leaves in bite-size pieces into salad bowl.

3. Arrange the other vegetables in groups on spinach. Refrigerate, covered, about 2 hours.

4. To serve: Remove garlic from dressing, and shake vigorously. Pour dressing over salad; toss until spinach is well coated. Serve at once.

Makes 6 to 8 servings.

Soups

Italians love soup, and their soups are inventive and excellent. A cup of broth, or brodo, often starts a meal, and a hearty minestrone, filled with vegetables and pasta, can be the main dish of a light evening meal. Unless it is brodo, soup is not served at the same meal with pasta or risotto. Traditionally, soup is served in deep plates.

Soups are made from whatever vegetables are plentiful, simmered in meat or vegetable stock. In the north they are thickened with rice, while farther south they contain the small pasta that are made especially for soups. These pastas are alfabeto (alphabet shapes), anellini (small rings), acini di pepe (pepper seeds, the smallest pasta), quadruccini (small squares), semini di melo (little seeds), stellette (little stars), nocchette (bows), conchigliette (little shells). Grated Parmesan or Romano cheese is added to soup individually at the table; cream soups are the only ones not served with cheese.

There are three kinds of Italian soups: broth, plain or with diced vegetables or a little pasta or rice, or with an egg beaten in just before serving (stracciatella); the hearty soups, a meal in themselves; and cream soups which are not so popular. Acceptable soups in the Italian tradition can be quickly concocted from canned bouillon or meat stock cubes and leftovers—meat or chicken, vegetables, dried beans, and pasta.

Vegetable Bouillon

ZUPPA D'ORTO

1 can (10½ ounces) condensed
  beef bouillon, undiluted
2 cans (12-ounce size)
  vegetable-juice cocktail

Dash pepper
6 parsley sprigs

1. In medium saucepan, combine bouillon, vegetable juice, and pepper. Over medium heat, bring just to boiling.

2. Serve in cups, each garnished with a parsley sprig.
Makes 6 servings.

Chicken Broth

BRODO DI POLLO

1 stewing chicken with giblets
2½ quarts water
1 large onion, quartered
3 carrots, sliced
4 stalks celery with leaves,
  chopped

2 leeks, sliced
2 fresh tomatoes, quartered
6 sprigs parsley
1 teaspoon salt
¼ teaspoon pepper

1. Place chicken and giblets in soup pot and add water. Bring slowly to a boil and remove scum from top of water.

2. Add onion, carrots, celery, leeks, tomatoes, parsley, salt, and pepper. Cover and simmer for 2½ hours.

3. Remove chicken and save for other recipes.

4. Continue cooking broth for 1 hour. Correct seasoning, then strain.
Makes 6 servings.

Roman "Ragged" Egg Soup

STRACCIATELLA

5 cups chicken broth
2 eggs

4 tablespoons grated Parmesan
  cheese or 2½ tablespoons
  grated Romano

1. Heat chicken broth but do not let it boil.

2. Beat eggs with fork. Add cheese and mix well. Beat in 3 to 4 tablespoons hot broth.

3. Slowly pour egg mixture into hot broth, stirring continuously. Allow soup to come just to boiling point, when eggs will have set into "ragged" strands. Serve at once.

Makes 4 to 6 servings.

Pasta and Bean Soup

ZUPPA DI PASTA E FAGIOLI

This hearty, family-style soup is a meal in itself. In the winter, slices of hard, dry sausage are simmered for ½ hour with the soup, and it is served with fresh bread and a rough red wine as the main course. In the summer, the soup is made with more water (8 to 10 cups) so that it is thinner. The pasta is omitted, and chopped fresh tomatoes are added just before serving.

1 cup dried white beans	1 clove garlic, crushed
6 cups water	1 stalk celery, chopped
1 ham knuckle or 3-inch cube	1 teaspoon salt
salt pork	¼ teaspoon pepper
2 tablespoons olive oil	½ cup soup pasta
2 onions, chopped	1 tablespoon chopped parsley

1. Soak beans in cold water to cover overnight.

2. Drain beans and place in deep pot with 6 cups water and ham knuckle. Cover and simmer for 1½ to 3 hours, or until beans are tender.

3. Purée half the cooked beans in a blender or food mill. Return purée to soup pot.

4. Heat oil and sauté onions, garlic, and celery until soft, about 10 minutes. Add to bean mixture. Season soup with salt and pepper. Continue cooking soup for 30 minutes to blend flavors. If soup is too thick, add more water.

5. Just before serving, add pasta to soup and cook until pasta is just tender. Pour soup into tureen and sprinkle with parsley.

Makes 6 servings.

Seafood Soup

ZUPPA DI PESCE

4 dozen clams, scrubbed	2 pounds firm fish fillets
1 2-pound live lobster	¼ cup olive oil
10 pieces frozen crab legs	2 onions, chopped

4 cloves garlic, minced
4 fresh tomatoes, peeled and
  chopped
1 cup dry white wine
1½ cups boiling water
¼ teaspoon saffron
1 bay leaf

1 teaspoon salt
¼ teaspoon freshly ground black
  pepper
1 tablespoon butter
6 slices Italian bread, browned
  in olive oil
1 tablespoon chopped parsley

1. Prepare shellfish and fish. Make sure clams are well scrubbed. Cut lobster into 6 pieces. Cut fish fillets into large pieces. Cod, haddock, red snapper, mullet, mackerel, and sole are suitable choices. Include at least two different kinds of fish in the soup.

2. Heat olive oil in deep pot and add onions, garlic, and tomatoes. Sauté for 5 minutes, then add wine. Simmer for additional 5 minutes.

3. Add fish and shellfish, boiling water, saffron, bay leaf, salt, and pepper. Cover and cook for 15 minutes, or until fish fillets are tender.

4. Place fish and shellfish in a heated serving bowl.

5. Swirl butter into hot soup. Place slice of bread in each soup plate and pour soup over it. Sprinkle soup with parsley. Pass the bowl of seafood separately.

Makes 6 servings.

Spring Soup

MINESTRA PRIMAVERILE

2 tablespoons butter
1 large onion, chopped
2 stalks celery with leaves,
  chopped
6 cups chicken or beef broth
1 medium zucchini, thinly sliced

1 package (10 ounces) frozen
  green peas
3 tomatoes, peeled and chopped
6 frozen artichoke hearts,
  sliced in half
½ cup soup pasta

1. Heat butter and sauté onion and celery in it until soft.

2. Add onions and celery to broth and bring to a boil. Add zucchini, peas, tomatoes, artichoke hearts, and pasta. Cook for 10 minutes.

3. Serve soup from a tureen and pass grated Parmesan cheese.

Makes 6 servings.

Italian Soup

MINESTRONE

Each region has its own variation of minestrone. In Genoa peas, turnips, and spinach are included, the pasta is ziti, a small elbow macaroni, and it is flavored with the basil pesto sauce just before serving. Green beans are typical of Tuscany. During the summer in Milan, minestrone is served semi-freddo, or lukewarm.

3-pound shin of beef	1 can (1 pound, 4 ounces) chick-
Salt	peas or kidney beans, undrained
4 quarts water	1 package (10 ounces) frozen
4 medium carrots, pared	cut green beans
4 sprigs parsley	1 package (10 ounces) frozen peas
2 large celery stalks, cut up	2 cups chopped cabbage
1 large onion, quartered	¼ pound perciatelli or spaghetti,
1 bay leaf	broken into 1-inch pieces
1 can (1 pound, 1 ounce)	¼ teaspoon pepper
Italian tomatoes, undrained	

1. Place shin of beef, 1 tablespoon salt, and water in large kettle. Bring to boiling, covered; then skim surface.

2. Add carrots, parsley, celery, onion, and bay leaf; simmer, uncovered, 3 hours.

3. Remove beef and carrots; set aside. Strain broth—there should be about 7 cups.

4. In kettle, combine broth, tomatoes, chick-peas, green beans, peas, cabbage, perciatelli, 2 teaspoons salt, and the pepper; bring to boiling, stirring occasionally. Then reduce heat and simmer, covered, 45 minutes.

5. Meanwhile, slice carrots and cut meat from bone into small pieces. Add the meat to the simmering soup.

Makes 3½ quarts.

Stockpot Vegetable Soup

MINESTRA ALLA PAESANA

2 cans (10¾-ounce size)	½ cup julienne carrot strips*
condensed vegetable-and-beef	½ cup julienne celery strips*
stockpot soup	½ cup fresh or frozen peas
2⅔ cups water	

1. In medium saucepan, combine undiluted soup with water; heat to boiling.

* *One inch long; thin as matchsticks.*

2. Add vegetables; cook, covered, 10 minutes, or until vegetables are tender.

3. Ladle into bowls.

Makes 4 to 6 servings.

Note: If you wish, use ⅔ cup red wine instead of ⅔ cup of the water.

Cream of Artichoke Soup

CREMA DI CARCIOFI

2 large artichokes (about 1½ pounds)	3 tablespoons finely chopped onion
2 tablespoons lemon juice	3 tablespoons flour
3 cups canned clear chicken broth	½ teaspoon salt
3 tablespoons butter or margarine	⅛ teaspoon pepper
	⅛ teaspoon dried thyme leaves
	1 cup light cream

1. Trim stalks from base of artichokes; remove any discolored leaves. Wash well under cold water; drain.

2. Halve the artichokes lengthwise; remove choke and purplish inner leaves.

3. In a 3½-quart saucepan, combine artichokes, lemon juice, and chicken broth; bring to boiling. Reduce heat; simmer, covered, for 30 minutes, or until the artichokes are tender.

4. Meanwhile, in hot butter in medium saucepan, sauté onion until tender—about 5 minutes.

5. Stir flour into onion mixture; cook, stirring constantly, 5 to 8 minutes, or until onion and flour are a deep-golden color. Set aside.

6. Remove artichokes from broth; reserve broth.

7. Peel leaves from artichokes; dice hearts. With teaspoon, scrape fleshy portion from base of leaves; discard leaves.

8. Strain broth into flour mixture, stirring to make a smooth mixture. Add diced hearts and fleshy portion of artichokes, salt, pepper, and thyme; mix well.

9. Bring mixture to boiling. Reduce heat; simmer 3 minutes, or until slightly thickened.

10. Remove from heat. Stir in cream.

Makes about 1 quart.

Egg Dishes

Simple egg dishes are frequently served for lunch or supper, but eggs are never part of an Italian breakfast. Frittata, a firm and thoroughly cooked omelet, browned on both sides and served flat, is the most popular way of preparing eggs. A frittata includes diced vegetables or meat and is a fine way of using leftovers. With a salad, a glass of wine, cheese or fruit, and coffee, it makes a light and quickly prepared meal.

Another very popular way of cooking eggs is uova al tegamino, eggs fried in olive oil and then served in the skillet in which they were cooked so that they stay warm. Scrambled eggs, flavored with Parmesan cheese or fresh herbs or strips of prosciutto, is the other chief way Italians prepare eggs.

Olive Omelet

FRITTATA DI OLIVE

6 eggs
¼ teaspoon chili powder
1 teaspoon salt
1 tablespoon olive oil
¼ cup sliced, pitted ripe olives

2 tablespoons finely chopped pimiento
2 tablespoons finely chopped green pepper

1. In medium bowl, with rotary beater or wire whisk, beat eggs with chili powder, salt, and 2 tablespoons cold water just until well combined, not frothy.

2. Meanwhile, slowly heat oil in a 9-inch heavy skillet or omelet pan with a heat-resistant handle.

3. Add olives, pimiento, and green peppers to eggs; mix well. Turn mixture into skillet.

4. As eggs set, run spatula under edge to loosen, tilting pan to let uncooked portion run underneath. Continue cooking until bottom is golden brown and eggs are just set.

5. Run under broiler, 6 inches from heat, until top is golden—about 2 minutes.

6. Lift out onto serving platter; do not fold. Cut into pie-shape wedges. Makes 4 servings.

Spinach Omelet
FRITTATA DI SPINACI

3 tablespoons olive oil	⅓ cup grated Parmesan cheese
½ cup thinly sliced onion	1 tablespoon chopped parsley
10 eggs	1 small clove garlic, crushed
1 cup finely chopped raw	1 teaspoon salt
spinach (½ pound)	¼ teaspoon pepper

1. Preheat oven to 350°F. Heat oil in 10-inch heavy skillet with heat-resistant handle. Add onion; sauté until onion is tender and golden brown —about 5 minutes.

2. In large bowl, combine remaining ingredients; with wire whisk or fork, beat until well blended. Turn into skillet with onion.

3. Cook over low heat, lifting from bottom with a spatula as the eggs set—3 minutes.

4. Bake, uncovered, 10 minutes, or until top is set. With spatula, loosen from bottom and around edge, and slide onto serving platter. Cut into wedges.

Makes 4 to 6 servings.

Potato Omelet
FRITTATA DI PATATE

1 cup packaged sliced potatoes	1 clove garlic, peeled
¼ cup butter, margarine, or	6 eggs
bacon fat	1 teaspoon salt
⅓ cup sliced onion	⅛ teaspoon pepper

1. Preheat oven to 350°F. In small saucepan, add enough cold water to potatoes to cover; bring to boiling. Reduce heat and simmer, covered, 10 minutes, or until just tender. Drain well.

2. In an omelet pan or medium skillet with heat-resistant handle, melt 2 tablespoons butter. Add onion and garlic; sauté until golden—about 5 minutes.

3. Add potatoes and remaining butter; sauté until light golden—about 5 minutes. Remove garlic and discard.

4. Meanwhile, beat eggs with salt and pepper just to mix well, not foamy. Pour over potato mixture; cook slowly, lifting bottom part as it cooks to let uncooked portion flow underneath.

5. Bake 2 minutes, or until surface is golden. Invert onto heated serving platter.

Makes 4 servings.

Bologna and Eggs

FRITTATA ALLA BOLOGNESE

4 bologna slices (4 inches wide)	⅛ teaspoon salt
2 teaspoons butter or margarine	Parsley sprigs or watercress
4 eggs	

1. Slowly heat 9-inch heavy skillet or omelet pan with a heat-resistant handle. Remove outer casing from bologna slices. In hot butter, arrange bologna slices evenly in skillet; sauté slices on one side only.

2. In medium bowl, with rotary beater, beat eggs with salt and 1 tablespoon water, just until well mixed, but not very frothy. Then pour the beaten-egg mixture over and around the sautéed bologna slices in skillet.

3. Let eggs cook, without stirring, over low heat, just until they are set on the bottom. Broil, 6 inches from heat, until the top is set and golden—about 1 minute.

4. Run a metal spatula around edge of pan. Carefully slide out (without folding) onto heated platter. Garnish with parsley sprigs or watercress.

Makes 2 servings.

Italian-style Fried Eggs

UOVA FRITTE ALL'ITALIANA

¼ cup olive oil	Freshly ground black pepper
4 eggs	2 tablespoons grated Parmesan
½ teaspoon salt	cheese

1. Divide the olive oil between two small frying pans that can go into the oven. Heat the oil.

2. Break 2 eggs into each pan. Fry eggs slowly over low heat.

3. Remove pans from heat when whites are almost set. Sprinkle eggs with salt, pepper, and cheese.

4. Bake eggs in 400°F. oven for 5 minutes, or until cheese has melted. Serve eggs in frying pans.

Makes 2 servings.

Eggs with Chicken Livers

UOVA AL PIATTO ALL'EMILIANA

¼ cup butter	Freshly ground black pepper
4 eggs	3 tablespoons Marsala
6 chicken livers	12 canned asparagus spears
½ teaspoon salt	

1. Preheat the oven to 350°F. Melt half the butter in a shallow oven-proof baking dish.

2. Break eggs into baking dish. Cover and cook in oven for 10 minutes, or until lightly set.

3. Meanwhile, cut chicken livers into quarters. Heat remaining butter and cook livers for 1 to 2 minutes. Season with salt and pepper and add Marsala. Simmer for 5 minutes.

4. Heat asparagus spears.

5. Spoon chicken-liver mixture over the eggs. Garnish with asparagus spears, and serve at once in baking dish.

Makes 4 servings.

Eggs in Tomato Sauce

UOVA AFFOGATE IN POMODORO

¼ cup olive oil	1 teaspoon salt
1 onion, chopped	¼ teaspoon dried red pepper
2½ cups canned Italian tomatoes	flakes
1 tablespoon minced fresh basil or parsley	6 eggs

1. Heat olive oil in large frying pan. Add onion and cook until soft and transparent.

2. Add tomatoes, basil, salt, and pepper flakes to onions. Cover and simmer for 30 minutes.

3. One at a time, break the eggs carefully into the sauce. Cover pan and cook eggs slowly for 7 minutes, or until whites are set. Serve at once. Makes 6 servings.

Eggs Florentine

UOVA ALLA FIORENTINA

This elegant way of preparing eggs in little nests of spinach may also use individual casseroles.

2 packages (10-ounce size) frozen chopped spinach	⅓ cup grated Parmesan cheese
1½ teaspoons salt	1½ tablespoons flour
2 tablespoons light cream	Dash pepper
3 tablespoons butter or margarine	⅛ teaspoon nutmeg
	1 cup milk
	6 eggs

1. Preheat oven to 350°F. Butter an 8-by-8-by-2-inch baking dish.

2. Cook spinach as package label directs. Drain very well. Add 1 teaspoon salt, cream, and 1 tablespoon butter; mix well.

3. Turn spinach into prepared baking dish, to make an even layer; make 6 small depressions in spinach, spacing evenly. Sprinkle with 2 tablespoons grated cheese.

4. Melt remaining butter in small saucepan; remove from heat. Add flour, rest of salt, pepper, and nutmeg, stirring until smooth.

5. Gradually stir in milk; bring to boiling, stirring. Reduce heat, and simmer 1 minute.

6. Carefully break an egg into each depression in spinach. Spoon sauce completely over top. Sprinkle with rest of cheese.

7. Bake, uncovered, 15 minutes, or until eggs are set and top is golden. Makes 6 servings.

Florentine Egg and Veal Rolls

UOVA IN UMIDO ALLA FIORENTINA

4 thin veal scallops	1½ tablespoons butter
4 thin slices prosciutto	1 sprig fresh rosemary or
4 hard-cooked eggs, shelled	½ teaspoon dried
1 tablespoon olive oil	4 tablespoons white wine

1 tablespoon tomato paste   ¼ teaspoon pepper
¼ cup boiling water   Parsley sprigs
½ teaspoon salt

1. Pound the veal scallops with a mallet until each is large and thin enough to wrap around an egg.

2. Lay veal scallops flat and cover with prosciutto. Place an egg in the center of each veal-prosciutto slice. Wrap meat around egg with veal on the outside and tuck in ends. Tie each roll in the middle with white butcher's string.

3. Heat oil, butter, and rosemary in heavy frying pan. Cook egg rolls slowly until lightly browned on all sides.

4. Add wine, turn up heat, and cook until wine is reduced by half.

5. Thin tomato paste with boiling water and add to frying pan with salt and pepper. Cover and simmer for 1 hour, or until meat is tender.

6. Remove egg rolls from pan and cool. Remove string ties and cut each roll in half. Arrange on serving platter and garnish with parsley.

Makes 4 servings.

Pasta & Rice

PASTA

The basic food for two thirds of the Italian peninsula is pasta. In one of its over one hundred different varieties, pasta with olive oil and garlic or a sauce is an important part of the daily diet in the central and southern provinces. It is filling, inexpensive, quickly prepared, and combines with and stretches more expensive foods like meat and seafood.

Pasta—spaghetti and noodles—can be made at home; it is a simple but time-consuming project. However, the results are worth the effort it takes. Most Italian cooks make their own pasta. The recipe in this chapter for Fettuccine alla Alfredo requires homemade noodles and is an example of how delicious pasta can be. The quality of commercial pasta varies; the best is imported from Italy. Good quality pasta is a warm, ivory color and poor quality is a dirty white; there is also green pasta which is flavored with spinach. It is worth spending a little more to buy the best quality pasta.

Pasta is served as a first course or as the main dish of the meal. If it is to be the main dish, it should have a rich sauce and be preceded by a light antipasto, and followed by a green salad, fruit, and coffee. Pasta as a first course should be followed by simply prepared meat, a green vegetable and salad, and again dessert should be fruit. Red wine is served with rich, meat-sauced pasta, and white with delicately seasoned pasta.

There are two kinds of pasta: spaghetti and macaroni, and noodles. They come in innumerable sizes and shapes and lend themselves to as many different kinds of sauces. Spaghetti and macaroni are made from wheat flour with egg and water. Spaghetti is a round strand of dough; the best-known shapes are spaghettini, vermicelli, and spaghetti, the thickest of the solid-strand pasta. Macaroni comes as rigatoni, ziti (elbow macaroni is the smallest version of ziti), ditali, and the many shaped pasta such as farfalle, lumache, and conchiglie. Noodles are made of a pasta that is much richer with eggs than the spaghetti dough; consequently, noodle pasta is more fragile and less resilient to the touch. It comes in flat, narrow ribbons: linguine, taglierini, fettuccine, tagliatelle, and the much broader lasagne. It is cut into squares for the stuffed pasta, ravioli and tortellini, and little shapes for soup (see page 30).

Spaghetti with Tomato Sauce

SPAGHETTI AL POMODORO

Tomato Sauce
¼ cup olive or salad oil
¼ cup finely chopped onion
¼ cup finely chopped green
   pepper
2 cloves garlic, finely chopped
1 can (1 pound, 12 ounces)
   whole tomatoes, undrained
1 can (8 ounces) tomato sauce
1 teaspoon salt

¼ teaspoon pepper
½ teaspoon dried oregano leaves
½ teaspoon dried basil leaves
2 teaspoons sugar

1 package (8 ounces) spaghetti
3 quarts boiling water
1 tablespoon salt
Grated Parmesan cheese

1. Make Tomato Sauce: In the hot oil in medium saucepan, sauté the onion, green pepper, and garlic until golden and tender, about 10 minutes, stirring occasionally.

2. Add tomatoes, tomato sauce, salt, pepper, oregano, basil, and sugar; stir, with wooden spoon, to break up the tomatoes slightly.

3. Over medium heat, bring the mixture just to boiling. Reduce heat; simmer, covered, 40 minutes, stirring it occasionally.

4. Remove cover; simmer sauce, uncovered, for 20 minutes, or until slightly thickened.

5. Meanwhile, cook spaghetti in 3 quarts boiling water with 1 tablespoon salt, uncovered, until just tender—8 to 10 minutes. Turn spaghetti into colander; drain well.

6. Serve the spaghetti at once, with the sauce poured over. Sprinkle with grated Parmesan cheese.

Makes 4 to 6 servings.

Spaghetti and Meatballs Napoli

SPAGHETTI ALLA NAPOLETANA

Meatballs
2 eggs
½ cup milk
3 slices whole wheat bread,
    crumbled
¾ pound ground beef
½ pound ground pork
¼ pound ground veal
1 medium onion, finely chopped
⅓ cup finely chopped green
    pepper
2 tablespoons chopped parsley
1 large clove garlic, crushed
1 teaspoon salt
½ teaspoon pepper
Dash ground cloves
Dash nutmeg

Sauce
½ pound round steak
¼ pound salt pork
1 clove garlic
¼ cup white wine
1 can (1 pound, 12 ounces)
    whole tomatoes, undrained
1 can (6 ounces) tomato paste
2 tablespoons chopped parsley
1 teaspoon salt
¼ teaspoon pepper
¼ teaspoon dried basil leaves

1 package (1 pound) spaghetti
½ cup grated Parmesan cheese

1. Make Meatballs: Preheat oven to 450°. In medium bowl, beat eggs slightly. Add milk and bread; mix well. Let stand 5 minutes.

2. Add rest of meatball ingredients; mix well until well blended.

3. Shape into 12 balls—they'll be about 2½ inches in diameter. Place in a well-greased shallow baking pan.

4. Bake, uncovered, 15 minutes. Brush meatballs with pan drippings; bake 15 minutes longer.

5. Meanwhile, make Sauce: Wipe round steak with damp paper towels. Cut into ½-inch chunks. Set aside.

6. Chop salt pork in little pieces. Place in Dutch oven with garlic; sauté until well browned. Add beef, and brown on all sides.

7. Add wine; simmer, covered, 10 minutes.

8. Stir in tomatoes, tomato paste, ½ cup water, parsley, salt, pepper, and basil; bring to boiling. Reduce heat, and simmer, uncovered, ½ hour.

9. Add meatballs; simmer, covered and stirring occasionally, 1 hour longer.

10. Cook spaghetti as package label directs. Drain.

11. To serve: Place spaghetti on serving dish; top with meatballs and sauce, and sprinkle with grated Parmesan cheese.

Makes 6 servings.

Spaghetti with Tuna-Tomato Sauce

SPAGHETTI ALLA SALSA DI TONNO

½ pound spaghetti
1 package (1½ ounces) spaghetti-
   sauce mix
2 tablespoons salad oil
1 can (6 ounces) tomato paste

1 teaspoon sugar
1 can (7 ounces) solid-pack
   tuna, flaked and drained
Chopped parsley
Grated Parmesan cheese

1. Cook spaghetti as package label directs.

2. Meanwhile, prepare spaghetti-sauce mix with oil, tomato paste, and water as package label directs. Simmer 10 minutes. Add sugar and flaked tuna. Heat mixture 1 minute.

3. Drain spaghetti; divide onto 3 or 4 heated plates. Spoon sauce over top. Sprinkle with parsley and Parmesan.

Makes 3 or 4 servings.

Baked Ziti Casserole

ZITI AL FORNO

Sauce
¼ cup olive or salad oil
1 cup finely chopped onion
1 clove garlic, crushed
1 can (2 pounds, 3 ounces)
   Italian tomatoes, undrained
1 can (6 ounces) tomato paste
2 tablespoons chopped parsley
1 tablespoon salt
1 tablespoon sugar
1 teaspoon dried oregano leaves
½ teaspoon dried basil leaves
¼ teaspoon pepper
1 package (1 pound) ziti
   macaroni

Cheese Layer
2 cartons (15-ounce size) ricotta
   cheese
1 package (8 ounces) mozzarella
   cheese, diced
⅓ cup grated Parmesan cheese
2 eggs
1 tablespoon chopped parsley
1 teaspoon salt
¼ teaspoon pepper

3 tablespoons grated Parmesan
   cheese

1. Make Sauce: In hot oil in 6-quart kettle, sauté onion and garlic until golden brown—about 10 minutes. Add undrained tomatoes, tomato paste, 1½ cups water, 2 tablespoons parsley, 1 tablespoon salt, sugar, the oregano, basil, and ¼ teaspoon pepper; mix well, mashing tomatoes with fork.

2. Bring to boiling; reduce heat; simmer, covered and stirring occasionally, 1 hour.

3. Preheat oven to 350°F. Cook ziti as package label directs.

4. Make Cheese Layer: In large bowl, combine ricotta, mozzarella, ⅓ cup Parmesan, the eggs, parsley, salt, and pepper. Beat with wooden spoon until blended.

5. Spoon a little sauce into a 5-quart casserole. Layer a third of ziti, cheese mixture, and remaining sauce. Sprinkle sauce with 1 tablespoon Parmesan. Repeat twice.

6. Bake, uncovered, 45 minutes, or until bubbling in center.

Makes 8 to 10 servings.

Note: If desired, make casserole ahead, and refrigerate. Remove from refrigerator while preheating oven. Bake 60 minutes, or until heated through.

Macaroni with Beans

PASTA E FAGIOLI

½ cups dried navy or pea beans	1 clove garlic, crushed
Salt	2 cups diced, peeled tomatoes
½ package (1-pound size) shell	(1 pound)
macaroni (3 cups)	1 teaspoon dried sage leaves
3 tablespoons olive oil	½ teaspoon dried oregano leaves
1 large onion, chopped	¼ teaspoon pepper
2 cups sliced carrot	Chopped parsley
1 cup chopped celery	Grated Parmesan cheese

1. In a large bowl, combine beans with 6 cups cold water. Refrigerate overnight.

2. Next day, turn beans and water into 6-quart kettle. Add 1½ teaspoons salt.

3. Bring to boiling; reduce heat, and simmer, covered, about 3 hours, or until beans are tender. Stir several times during cooking. Drain, reserving liquid (there will be about 2½ cups).

4. Cook macaroni following package label directions.

5. Meanwhile, in hot oil in large skillet, sauté onion, carrot, celery, and garlic, covered, until soft—about 20 minutes. Do not brown. Add tomatoes, sage, oregano, ½ teaspoon salt, and the pepper. Cover; cook, over medium heat, 15 minutes.

6. In large saucepan or kettle, combine beans, macaroni, and sautéed vegetables. Add 1½ cups reserved bean liquid. Bring to boiling; cover;

simmer 35 to 40 minutes, stirring several times and adding more bean liquid if needed. Add salt and pepper if needed.

7. Turn into attractive serving dish or casserole. Sprinkle with chopped parsley and grated Parmesan cheese.

Makes 8 servings.

Homemade Ravioli with Italian Tomato Sauce

RAVIOLI ALLA CASALINGA

Italian Tomato Sauce, page 48	⅛ teaspoon pepper
	Noodle Dough
Ravioli Filling	3 cups unsifted all-purpose flour
1 carton (15 ounces) ricotta cheese	4 eggs
1 package (8 ounces) mozzarella cheese, diced	3 to 4 tablespoons water
¼ cup grated Parmesan cheese	2 tablespoons salt
1 egg	2 tablespoons olive or salad oil
1 tablespoon chopped parsley	
½ teaspoon salt	Grated Parmesan cheese

1. Make Italian Tomato Sauce as directed.

2. Meanwhile, make Ravioli Filling: In medium bowl, combine all filling ingredients. Beat with wooden spoon until well blended. Set aside.

3. Make Noodle Dough: Measure flour into medium bowl; make well in center. Add eggs and water. Beat with wooden spoon until dough forms ball and leaves side of bowl.

4. Turn out onto floured surface. Knead until smooth and elastic—6 to 8 minutes. Divide in quarters.

5. On lightly floured surface, roll one quarter (keep remaining dough covered with plastic film) into 17-by-13-inch rectangle. Cover with plastic film.

6. Roll a second quarter into a 17-by-13-inch rectangle. Drop filling by teaspoonfuls in 24 evenly spaced mounds on this dough rectangle (6 lengthwise and 4 across). Set remaining filling aside. Place first dough rectangle on top; trim edges with pastry wheel. Run pastry wheel between mound of filling to make 24 ravioli; press edges of each with tines of fork to seal.

7. Place on flour-covered sheet of waxed paper to dry—about 15 minutes. Turn once.

8. Repeat with remaining dough and filling.

9. In large kettle, bring 8 quarts water to boiling. Add salt, oil, and ravioli. Boil gently, covered, 15 to 20 minutes, or until done. Turn half of ravioli into colander at one time; drain very well.

10. Turn ravioli into large heated serving dish. Top with some tomato sauce; pass remaining sauce. Sprinkle ravioli with Parmesan.

Makes 8 to 10 servings.

Italian Tomato Sauce
1 can (2 pounds, 3 ounces) Italian tomatoes, undrained
¼ cup olive or salad oil
1 cup finely chopped onion
1 clove garlic, crushed
1 can (6 ounce) tomato paste
2 sprigs parsley
1 tablespoon salt
2 teaspoons sugar
1 teaspoon dried oregano leaves
½ teaspoon dried basil leaves
¼ teaspoon pepper

1. Purée undrained Italian tomatoes in electric blender.

2. In hot oil in large saucepan, sauté onion and garlic until golden brown—about 5 minutes.

3. Add puréed tomato, tomato paste, 1½ cups water, the parsley sprigs, salt, sugar, oregano, basil, and pepper; mix well.

4. Bring to boiling; reduce heat and simmer, covered and stirring occasionally, 1 hour.

Makes 5 cups.

Buttered Linguine Parmesan

LINGUINE ALLA PARMIGIANA

1 package (1 pound) linguine
¾ cup butter or margarine
2 tablespoons finely chopped onion
1 small clove garlic, crushed
2 tablespoons chopped parsley
½ cup grated Parmesan cheese

1. Cook linguine as package label directs.

2. Meanwhile, melt butter in small saucepan. Add onion and garlic, simmer 5 minutes. Keep warm.

3. Drain linguine, and place on serving platter. Pour sauce over all; sprinkle with parsley; toss gently. Sprinkle with Parmesan and serve immediately.

Makes 8 servings.

Buttered Green and White Noodles

FETTUCCINE VERDI NATURALI

Salt	¾ cup butter or margarine,
1 package (8 ounces) green	melted
noodles	½ teaspoon dried basil leaves
1 package (8 ounces) medium	½ teaspoon dried oregano leaves
noodles	⅛ teaspoon pepper
¾ teaspoon salt	½ cup grated Parmesan cheese

1. In large kettle, bring 6 quarts water and 2 tablespoons salt to boiling.

2. Add both kinds of noodles; bring to boiling; cook, stirring occasionally, 7 to 10 minutes, or just until noodles are tender.

3. Drain noodles; return to kettle. Add ¾ teaspoon salt, the melted butter, basil, oregano, and pepper; toss gently to combine.

4. Turn noodles onto platter; sprinkle with the grated Parmesan cheese. Makes 10 to 12 servings.

Noodles Alfredo

FETTUCCINE ALL'ALFREDO

Homemade Noodles	Alfredo Sauce
3 cups unsifted all-purpose flour	½ cup butter or margarine
Salt	⅔ cup heavy cream
3 eggs	1¼ cups grated Parmesan cheese
3 tablespoons lukewarm water	¼ teaspoon salt
	Dash pepper
	Chopped parsley

1. Make Homemade Noodles: In medium bowl, combine flour and ½ teaspoon salt. Make well in center. Add eggs and water; beat vigorously with fork until ingredients are well combined. Dough will be stiff.

2. Turn out on lightly floured surface, and knead until smooth and elastic—about 15 minutes. Cover with bowl; let rest 10 minutes. Then divide dough into 4 parts. Keep covered with bowl until ready to roll out.

3. Roll out each part to paper thinness, a 12-inch square. Sprinkle lightly with flour. Then roll loosely around rolling pin, as for jelly roll. Slip out rolling pin. With sharp knife, cut into ⅛-inch-wide strips for fine noodles, ⅓-inch-wide strips for broad noodles. Arrange the dough strips on an ungreased cookie sheet.

4. In large kettle, bring 4 quarts water with 1 tablespoon salt to boiling.

Add noodles; return to boiling. Boil, uncovered and stirring occasionally, until tender—about 20 to 25 minutes. Drain noodles; keep warm.

5. Make Alfredo Sauce: Heat butter and cream in medium saucepan until butter is melted. Remove from heat. Add 1 cup Parmesan cheese, the salt, and pepper. Stir until the sauce is blended and fairly smooth.

6. Add to drained noodles, and toss until they are well coated. Sprinkle with remaining Parmesan cheese and the chopped parsley. Serve at once. Makes 6 servings.

Baked Lasagne

LASAGNE AL FORNO

Lasagne makes a good main course for a family-style dinner party. Serve it with an antipasto of Pickled Garden Relish, a Green Salad, Zabaglione, chilled and poured over fresh peaches, and espresso coffee. Drink a light, sparkling red wine.

Tomato Sauce	2 teaspoons dried oregano leaves
¼ cup olive or salad oil	1 teaspoon dried basil leaves
½ cup finely chopped onion	¼ teaspoon pepper
1 clove garlic, crushed	
2 tablespoons chopped parsley	1 tablespoon salt
½ pound ground chuck	1 tablespoon olive or salad oil
¼ pound ground pork	½ package (1-pound size) lasagne
1 can (2 pounds, 3 ounces)	noodles
Italian tomatoes, undrained	1 pound ricotta cheese
2 cans (6-ounce size) tomato	1 pound mozzarella cheese,
paste	thinly sliced
2 tablespoons sugar	1 jar (3 ounces) grated Parmesan
1 tablespoon salt	cheese

1. Make Tomato Sauce: In ¼ cup hot oil in Dutch oven, sauté onion, garlic, and parsley until onion is tender—about 5 minutes.

2. Add chuck and pork; sauté until well browned. Add tomatoes, tomato paste, sugar, 1 tablespoon salt, the oregano, basil, and pepper; mix well, mashing tomatoes with fork.

3. Bring to boiling. Reduce heat and simmer, covered and stirring occasionally, 3 hours.

4. In large kettle, bring 3 quarts water and 1 tablespoon salt to boiling. Add 1 tablespoon olive oil. Add lasagne noodles, 2 or 3 pieces at a time. to the boiling water. Return to boiling; boil, uncovered and stirring occasionally, 15 minutes. Drain; rinse under hot water.

5. Preheat oven to 350°F. Grease a 13-by-9-by-2-inch baking dish.

6. Spoon a little tomato sauce into prepared dish. Layer noodles, ricotta, mozzarella, tomato sauce, and Parmesan. Repeat until all ingredients are used, ending with sauce and Parmesan.

7. Bake, uncovered, 45 to 50 minutes, or until cheese is melted and top is browned. Let stand 10 to 15 minutes before cutting, to make serving easier.

Makes 9 servings.

Shrimp Lasagne

LASAGNE AGLI SCAMPI

2 teaspoons salt	3 packages (7-ounce size) frozen
2 packages (6-ounce size)	shelled and deveined shrimp
Italian-style noodle mix	1 pound small-curd cottage
¼ cup butter or margarine	cheese
	¼ cup grated Parmesan cheese

1. Preheat oven to 375°F. Lightly grease 3-quart casserole.

2. In large saucepan, bring 2 quarts water to boiling. Add salt and noodles from both packages of mix.

3. Bring back to boiling; boil, uncovered, stirring occasionally, 5 minutes, or until noodles are tender.

4. Drain noodles well; do not rinse. Return to saucepan. Add butter, tomato-sauce mix from both packages of noodles, and 2⅔ cups hot water; toss to mix well.

5. Meanwhile, cook shrimp as package label directs; drain.

6. In prepared casserole, layer ⅓ tomato-noodle mixture, ½ shrimp, 1 packet of cheese filling from package of noodles, and ½ of cottage cheese. Repeat layering.

7. Top with rest of noodles. Sprinkle top with Parmesan cheese. Bake about 25 minutes, or until hot and bubbly.

Makes 6 to 8 servings.

Baked Manicotti

MANICOTTI AL FORNO

Manicotti is a good main dish for a dinner party menu, for it can be made ahead and then baked just before serving. Since it is easy to eat and doesn't require a knife, it is particularly suitable for a buffet dinner. A party menu might include Eggplant Appetizer, Cauliflower Salad, Biscuit Tortoni, Chianti, and espresso.

Sauce
¼ cup olive oil
1 cup finely chopped onion
1 clove garlic, crushed
1 can (2 pounds, 3 ounces) Italian tomatoes, undrained
1 can (6 ounces) tomato paste
2 sprigs parsley
1 tablespoon salt
2 teaspoons sugar
1 teaspoon dried oregano leaves
½ teaspoon dried basil leaves
¼ teaspoon pepper

Shells
5 eggs

1¼ cups unsifted all-purpose flour
¼ teaspoon salt
1 teaspoon butter or margarine

Filling
2 pounds ricotta cheese
1 package (8 ounces) mozzarella cheese, diced
⅓ cup grated Parmesan cheese
2 eggs
1 tablespoon chopped parsley
1 teaspoon salt
¼ teaspoon pepper

2 tablespoons grated Parmesan cheese

1. Make Sauce: In hot oil in 6-quart kettle, sauté onion and garlic until golden brown—about 5 minutes. Add tomatoes, tomato paste, 1½ cups water, parsley sprigs, 1 tablespoon salt, the sugar, oregano, basil, and ¼ teaspoon pepper; mix well, mashing tomatoes with fork.

2. Bring to boiling. Reduce heat; simmer, covered and stirring occasionally, 1 hour.

3. Meanwhile, make Shells: In medium bowl, combine 5 eggs, flour, ¼ teaspoon salt, and 1¼ cups water; with portable electric mixer, beat until smooth.

4. Melt butter in 7-inch skillet. Pour in 2 tablespoons batter, rotating pan quickly, to spread batter evenly over bottom of pan. Cook, over medium heat, until top is dry but bottom is not brown. Turn out on wire rack to cool.

5. Continue cooking batter, 2 tablespoons at a time, until all is used. As shells cool, stock them with waxed paper between them.

6. Preheat oven to 350°F.

7. Make Filling: In large bowl, combine ricotta, mozzarella, ⅓ cup Parmesan, 2 eggs, chopped parsley, 1 teaspoon salt, and ¼ teaspoon pepper; beat with wooden spoon until well blended.

8. Place about ¼ cup filling in center of each shell, and roll up.

9. Spoon some of sauce in bottom of two 13-by-9-by-2-inch baking

dishes. Place shells, seam side down, in single layer in dishes. Cover with remaining sauce; sprinkle with 2 tablespoons Parmesan.

10. Bake, uncovered, 30 minutes, or until bubbly.

Makes 8 to 10 servings.

The following sauces are suitable for almost any of the pastas.

Marinara Sauce

SALSA ALLA MARINARA

This "sailor's" sauce is good not only with pasta but with shrimp and lobster or poured over veal scallopine.

⅓ cup olive or salad oil
2 or 3 cloves garlic, crushed
⅓ cup chopped parsley

1 can (1pound, 12 ounces) Italian tomatoes, undrained
1 teaspoon dried oregano leaves
½ teaspoon salt
Dash pepper

1. In hot oil in large skillet, sauté garlic and parsley about 3 minutes. Add the tomatoes, oregano, salt, and pepper; mix well, mashing the tomatoes with a fork.

2. Bring the mixture to boiling. Then reduce heat and simmer, uncovered and stirring occasionally, for 30 minutes, or until the sauce is thickened.

Makes 2½ cups sauce, or enough for ½ pound spaghetti.

Garden-fresh Tomato Sauce

SALSA DI POMODORO

¼ cup olive or salad oil
2 medium onions, chopped
2 cloves garlic, split
¼ teaspoon dried basil leaves, or 1 teaspoon chopped fresh

2 teaspoons salt
2½ quarts chopped peeled tomatoes (4 pounds)
4 sprigs parsley
1 tablespoon sugar

1. Heat oil in Dutch oven or large saucepan. Add onion, garlic, basil, and salt; sauté until onion is tender—about 5 minutes. Discard garlic.

2. Stir in tomatoes, parsley, and sugar; bring to boiling. Reduce heat, and simmer, uncovered and stirring occasionally, 2 hours, or until sauce is thickened. Remove parsley.

Makes 6 cups sauce.

White Clam Sauce

SALSA DI VONGOLE

2 cans (7½-ounce size)
  minced clams
¼ cup olive or salad oil
¼ cup butter or margarine

2 cloves garlic, crushed
2 tablespoons chopped parsley
1½ teaspoons salt

1. Drain clams, reserving ¾ cup liquid. Set aside.
2. In skillet, slowly heat oil and butter. Add garlic, and sauté until golden. Remove from heat.
3. Stir in clam liquid, parsley, salt; bring to boiling. Reduce heat; simmer, uncovered, 10 minutes.
4. Add clams; simmer 3 minutes.
Makes about 1 cup sauce, or enough for ½ pound spaghetti.

Pesto Sauce

PESTO ALLA GENOVESE

This is a speciality of Genoa where it is served on spaghetti or stirred by the tablespoon into minestrone just before serving and after the soup has been taken off the heat. If fresh basil is available, use it by all means, for the flavor of the sauce will be incomparably better. Substitute ½ cup minced fresh basil leaves for the parsley, dried basil, and marjoram in the recipe. In Genoa pesto is pounded in a mortar and pestle until the right consistency is reached; if your kitchen has this equipment, try blending the ingredients the Italian way.

¼ cup butter or margarine,
  softened
¼ cup grated Parmesan cheese
½ cup finely chopped parsley
1 clove garlic, crushed

½ teaspoon dried basil leaves
¼ teaspoon dried marjoram leaves
¼ cup olive or salad oil
¼ cup finely chopped walnuts
  or pine nuts

1. With wooden spoon, cream butter, Parmesan, parsley, garlic, basil, and marjoram until well blended.
2. Gradually add oil, beating constantly. Add walnuts; mix well.
3. Add to spaghetti in heated serving dish, and toss until well coated. Makes about 1 cup sauce, or enough for ½ pound spaghetti.
Note: If desired, prepare sauce a day ahead, and refrigerate, covered. Before serving, let warm to room temperature, and mix well.

RICE
Riso

Rice is the starch of the north of Italy—the Piedmont, Lombardy, and Venice areas. It is seen on the table as frequently as pasta is farther south. The country is particularly suited to growing rice and the quality is excellent. Unless your local stores carry imported Italian rice, use either long- or short-grain Carolina rice in the following recipes.

Although rice is frequently added to soups, it is usually served as a risotto, a creamy combination of rice, vegetables, meat, or seafood, cooked in stock and served in shallow soup plates, although it is always eaten with a fork. Risotto is a course in itself, as is pasta, and is never served as an accompaniment to a meat or fish course. There is one exception to this rule, however, for risotto alla Milanese is traditionally served with osso buco, braised veal shanks, which are a specialty of Milan.

Savory Mushroom Rice

RISO IN BIANCO CON FUNGHI

3 tablespoons butter or margarine	½ teaspoon salt
1 cup raw long-grain white rice	⅛ teaspoon pepper
1 can (6 ounces) chopped mushrooms, drained and reserved	1 tablespoon chopped parsley

1. Melt butter in medium saucepan. Add rice; sauté over medium heat, stirring constantly, 5 minutes.

2. Drain mushroom liquid into 4-cup measure. Add mushrooms to rice.

3. Add water to mushroom liquid to measure 2½ cups. Add to rice with salt and pepper.

4. Bring to boiling; reduce heat; simmer, covered, 25 to 30 minutes, or until rice is tender and all liquid is absorbed.

5. To serve: Sprinkle parsley over top. Fluff rice with a fork. Turn out onto heated large serving platter.

Makes 6 servings.

Venetian Rice and Peas

RISI E BISI

6 tablespoons butter or margarine	1 cup raw long-grain white rice
⅓ cup finely chopped onion	1 package (10 ounces) frozen peas
2 tablespoons finely chopped parsley	1 teaspoon salt
	2 tablespoons grated Parmesan cheese

1. In 4 tablespoons hot butter in heavy, 3-quart saucepan, sauté onion and parsley 5 minutes. Add rice; sauté, stirring occasionally, 5 minutes.

2. Add 2 cups water. Bring to boiling; reduce heat, and simmer, covered, without stirring, 14 minutes, or until liquid is all absorbed.

3. Meanwhile, cook peas as package label directs; drain well.

4. Stir peas, salt, and remaining butter into rice. Turn into serving dish.

5. Sprinkle top with grated Parmesan cheese.

Makes 6 to 8 servings.

Saffron Rice

RISOTTO ALLA MILANESE

1 can (10½ ounces) condensed chicken broth, undiluted	½ cup finely chopped onion
⅛ teaspoon saffron	1 cup raw long-grain white rice
6 tablespoons butter or margarine	⅓ cup dry white wine
	⅓ cup grated Parmesan cheese

1. In small saucepan, heat chicken broth with saffron just until hot. Set aside.

2. In 4 tablespoons butter in heavy 3½-quart saucepan, sauté onion until tender—about 2 minutes. Add rice, and cook, stirring occasionally, until golden—about 5 minutes.

3. Add reserved chicken broth, ½ cup water, and the wine; bring to boiling. Reduce heat, and simmer, covered, 30 minutes, or until all liquid is absorbed.

4. Just before serving, stir in remaining 2 tablespoons butter and the Parmesan cheese.

Makes 6 servings.

Italian Rice and Sausage

RISOTTO CON SALICCE ALL'ITALIANA

1 pound sausage meat	½ teaspoon salt
1 cup chopped onion	⅛ teaspoon pepper
1 cup chopped celery	2 teaspoons bottled thick
1 cup sliced fresh mushrooms	steak sauce
1 cup raw long-grain white rice	⅓ cup grated Parmesan cheese
2 cups canned beef bouillon	¼ cup chopped pimiento

1. Preheat oven to 350°F.

2. In large skillet, sauté sausage, stirring, 5 minutes. Remove sausage with slotted spoon.

3. In drippings, sauté onion, celery, and mushrooms, stirring, 5 minutes.

4. Add rice; sauté, stirring, 5 minutes longer. Turn into ungreased 2-quart casserole.

5. Heat bouillon to boiling. Add to rice mixture, along with sausage, salt, pepper, steak sauce, cheese, and pimiento; mix well.

6. Bake, covered, 1 hour, or until rice is tender.

Makes 4 to 6 servings.

CORN MEAL

Polenta

Polenta is made of yellow corn meal and is similar to corn meal mush. It is a staple food in northern Italy, where it is eaten as a course in itself and served with meat, fish, or cheese sauces. Traditionally, polenta is cooked in a deep copper pot and stirred with a wooden spoon.

Italian Corn Meal Mush

POLENTA

1 tablespoon salt	2 cups yellow corn meal

1. In a 9- or 10-inch skillet, bring 4 cups water and the salt to a full, rolling boil.

2. Slowly add corn meal, stirring constantly with wire whisk—mixture will get very thick. With spatula, smooth top.

3. Turn heat very low, and cook, uncovered and without stirring, until thick crust forms around edge and mixture is firm—about 20 minutes.

4. To serve: With spatula, loosen around edge and underneath. Invert on large round platter.

Makes 6 to 8 servings.

DUMPLINGS

Gnocchi

Gnocchi, or dumplings of farina or mashed potatoes, is a typical everyday dish for Italians. It is served as rice or pasta would be. This recipe is how gnocchi is prepared in Rome; with a salad it is a good luncheon dish.

Farina Baked Dumplings

GNOCCHI ALLA ROMANA

3 cups milk	2 eggs, beaten
1 cup farina	½ cup grated Parmesan cheese
4 tablespoons butter or	½ teaspoon salt
margarine	Dash nutmeg

1. Lightly butter a 13-by-9-by-2-inch baking pan. Heat the milk slightly in a 3½-quart heavy saucepan; do not boil.

2. Sprinkle in farina. Cook, over medium heat and stirring, until mixture is thick—about 5 minutes. Remove from heat.

3. Stir in half of butter, the eggs, ¼ cup Parmesan, the salt, and nutmeg; beat until smooth. Spread evenly in prepared baking pan. Refrigerate until firm—about 3 hours.

4. To serve: Cut the chilled mixture into 24 pieces. Arrange pieces, overlapping, in shallow baking pan. Melt remaining butter, and sprinkle over top with remaining Parmesan.

5. Broil, 4 inches from heat, until hot and golden—about 5 minutes. Makes 8 servings.

Fish, Poultry & Meat

FISH
Pesce

Fish is plentiful in Italy and is an important part of the national diet. Much of the fish and seafood of the Mediterranean is unique, so it is impossible to duplicate many Italian staple dishes like their excellent fish soups and stews in this country. Firm-fleshed fish—mullet, sole, fresh tuna—is usually broiled or fried in olive oil with lemon juice and fresh herbs. The pink scampi of the Adriatic are neither shrimp nor lobster, but either one can substitute with delicious results in Italian scampi recipes.

Italian-Style Shrimp
SCAMPI

In this classic recipe, the best shrimp to use are the largest the fish market has.

1 pound large raw shrimp	2 tablespoons chopped parsley
½ cup butter or margarine	1 teaspoon grated lemon peel
½ teaspoon salt	1 tablespoon lemon juice
6 cloves garlic, crushed	Lemon wedges

1. Preheat oven to 400°F. Shell shrimp; leave on tails, with their shells. Devein. Wash under running water; drain on paper towels.

2. Melt butter in a 13-by-9-by-2-inch baking dish, in oven. Add salt, garlic, and 1 tablespoon parsley; mix well.

3. Arrange shrimp in single layer in baking dish; bake, uncovered, 5 minutes.

4. Turn shrimp. Sprinkle with lemon peel, lemon juice, and remaining parsley; bake 8 to 10 minutes longer, or just until tender.

5. Arrange shrimp on heated serving platter. Pour garlic-butter drippings over all. Garnish with lemon.

Makes 4 servings.

Shrimp Marinara with Rice

SCAMPI ALLA MARINARA CON RISOTTO

1 tablespoon salad oil	⅛ teaspoon pepper
2 cloves garlic, crushed	Dash cayenne
1 tablespoon chopped parsley	1 can (1 pound, 12 ounces)
1 tablespoon sugar	Italian tomatoes, undrained
1 teaspoon salt	2 pounds raw shrimp
½ teaspoon dried oregano leaves	4 cups hot cooked white rice
¼ teaspoon dried basil leaves	

1. Slowly heat oil in large, heavy skillet. Add garlic; sauté until golden—about 3 minutes.

2. Remove from heat; add parsley, sugar, salt, oregano, basil, pepper, cayenne, and tomatoes. Break up tomatoes with spoon; bring to boiling.

3. Reduce heat; simmer, uncovered, 25 minutes, stirring occasionally.

4. In large saucepan, cover shrimp with cold water; bring just to boiling. Drain shrimp; shell and devein.

5. Add shrimp to sauce; simmer, stirring, just until heated through—about 10 minutes.

6. To serve: Spoon rice around edge of large, round platter. Mound shrimp and sauce in center of platter.

Makes 8 servings.

Lobster with Marinara Sauce

ARAGOSTA ALLA MARINARA

Marinara Sauce	3 cups sliced fresh mushrooms
½ cup olive or salad oil	1 can (2 pounds, 3 ounces)
3 cloves garlic, split	Italian plum tomatoes,
1 cup chopped onion	undrained

2 teaspoons salt
½ teaspoon pepper
Dash ground cloves
½ teaspoon dried oregano leaves
¼ teaspoon dried basil leaves
1 tablespoon sugar

5 (5-ounce size) frozen rock-
    lobster tails, thawed
1 pound spaghetti
Grated Parmesan cheese
Chopped parsley
Lemon wedges

1. Make Marinara Sauce: In hot oil in 4-quart Dutch oven or kettle, brown garlic. Remove garlic and discard.

2. Add onion and mushrooms to oil; sauté, stirring, 10 minutes.

3. Add tomatoes, salt, pepper, cloves, oregano, basil, and sugar; mix well.

4. Bring to boiling; reduce heat, and boil gently, uncovered and stirring occasionally, 30 minutes.

5. Meanwhile, with kitchen shears, cut undershells from lobster tails, leaving top shell intact. Cut each tail crosswise, right through shell, into 3 pieces.

6. Add lobster pieces to sauce; simmer, uncovered, 20 minutes or until lobster is tender.

7. While lobster is simmering, cook spaghetti as package label directs. Drain.

8. To serve: Arrange spaghetti around edge of large platter. Spoon lobster and sauce into center. Sprinkle with Parmesan cheese and parsley. Serve with lemon wedges.

Makes 6 servings.

Tiny Lobster Tails, Broiled

CODE D'ARAGOSTA

2 packages (8-ounce size) tiny
    frozen rock-lobster tails,
    thawed
Skewers or hibachi sticks
1 teaspoon salt
⅓ cup olive oil
4 tablespoons chopped parsley

2 tablespoons chopped green
    onion
4 tablespoons butter or
    margarine
2 tablespoons lemon juice

Lemon wedges
Parsley sprigs

1. With scisors, cut away soft undershell of lobster tails. Push a skewer lengthwise into each lobster tail, to keep them from curling. Place lobster tails, shell side up, in broiler pan without rack.

2. Broil, 4 inches from heat, 2 minutes. Turn lobster tails meat side up, sprinkle with salt. Combine olive oil, 2 tablespoons chopped parsley, and the green onion, spoon on lobster meat. Broil 3 to 5 minutes, or until meat is opaque.

3. To serve: Loosen lobster meat from shells. Place tails on heated serving platter. Pour juices from broiler pan over tails. Keep warm.

4. In small saucepan, combine butter, lemon juice, and remaining chopped parsley; heat to boiling point. Pour over lobster tails. Garnish platter with lemon and parsley.

Makes 4 servings.

Lobster Fra Diavolo

ARAGOSTA FRA DIAVOLO

¼ cup olive or salad oil	1 teaspoon dried oregano leaves
1 clove garlic, chopped	½ teaspoon salt
1 can (1 pound, 1 ounce)	¼ teaspoon crushed red pepper
Italian tomatoes, undrained	2 (1½-pound size) live lobsters
2 tablespoons chopped parsley	

1. Preheat oven to 375°F.

2. In hot oil in medium saucepan, sauté garlic until golden—about 2 minutes. Add tomatoes, parsley, oregano, salt, and red pepper, and mix well, mashing the tomatoes with a fork.

3. Bring to boiling. Reduce heat, and simmer, uncovered, 10 minutes.

4. Meanwhile, kill lobsters: Lay each on back shell on wooden board. Insert sharp knife into back shell where head and body of lobster come together, to sever spinal cord.

5. Split down middle to end of tail, cutting through thin undershell just to back shell. Spread open. Tomalley (green liver) and coral parts are edible; but discard dark vein and small sac below head. Crack large claws.

6. Place lobsters, cut side up, in large, shallow baking pan. Cover evenly with tomato mixture.

7. Bake, uncovered, 25 minutes, or until lobster meat is tender. Serve with pan drippings as sauce. Garnish with parsley sprigs and lemon slices, if desired.

Makes 2 servings.

Fillet of Sole Florentine

SOGLIOLE ALLA FIORENTINA

Stuffing
1 package (10 ounces) frozen
  chopped spinach
4 tablespoons butter or
  margarine
½ cup chopped onion
2 cups soft bread crumbs
2 tablespoons grated Parmesan
  cheese
¼ teaspoon salt
Dash ground cloves

6 or 7 small sole or flounder
  fillets (about 2 pounds)

1 tablespoon lemon juice
1 teaspoon salt

Sauce
4 tablespoons butter or margarine
2 tablespoons flour
½ teaspoon salt
⅛ teaspoon pepper
¾ cup milk
½ cup dry white wine
2 egg yolks, slightly beaten

1. Make stuffing: Cook spinach as package label directs. Turn into a sieve; press down with spoon so it will drain thoroughly.

2. In 4 tablespoons hot butter in medium saucepan, sauté onion until tender—about 3 minutes. Add drained spinach, bread crumbs, Parmesan, ¼ teaspoon salt, and the cloves; toss until well combined.

3. Preheat oven to 375°F. Generously grease a 5½ cup ring mold.

4. Wash sole fillets, and dry well on paper towels. Brush with lemon juice; sprinkle both sides with salt—1 teaspoon in all. Arrange fillets, white side down, around side of prepared ring mold, letting ends hang over edge of mold. Fill mold with stuffing; fold ends of fillets over stuffing. Cover mold with foil.

5. Place mold in shallow baking pan. Pour hot water to ½-inch depth around mold.

6. Bake 35 minutes, or until fish flakes easily when tested with fork. Let stand 5 minutes; then carefully pour liquid from mold into 1-cup measure. Set aside. Cover mold with foil, and keep warm.

7. Make Sauce: Melt butter in small saucepan. Remove from heat. Stir in flour, salt, and pepper until smooth. Gradually stir in milk, ⅓ cup reserved fish liquid, and the wine. Bring to boiling, stirring constantly; boil gently 1 minute.

8. Stir a little of hot mixture into egg yolks, mixing well. Return to rest of hot mixture; cook, stirring, 1 minute longer.

9. Unmold fish ring, stuffing side down, on heated serving dish. Spoon some of sauce over fish, and pass remaining sauce in a bowl.

Makes 6 servings.

Baked Cod

BACCALA AL FORNO

In Italy salt cod is used in this recipe, but the dish is more delicate and appeals more to American tastes when made with frozen or fresh cod.

2 packages (12-ounce size) cod fillets, thawed	3 tablespoons dry white wine
½ teaspoon seasoned salt	1 tablespoon drained bottled capers
1 tablespoon lemon juice	Dash dried oregano leaves
1 can (8 ounces) spaghetti sauce with mushrooms	

1. Preheat oven to 400°F.

2. Arrange cod in a 12-by-8-by-2-inch baking dish. Sprinkle evenly with the seasoned salt and lemon juice.

3. In small saucepan, combine spaghetti sauce with wine, capers, and oregano. Bring to boiling; reduce heat and simmer, uncovered, 5 minutes.

4. Pour sauce over cod. Bake, uncovered, 15 to 20 minutes, or until cod flakes easily with fork.

Makes 4 servings.

Seafood en Papillote

FRUTTI DI MARE

6 fresh perch, pompano, or turbot (¾ pound each), cleaned, heads and tails removed	Dried marjoram leaves
	2 cloves garlic, peeled and slivered
12 mussels	Salt
12 littleneck clams	Pepper
12 fresh shrimp	3 teaspoons olive oil
12 fresh scallops	3 tablespoons lemon juice
Dried thyme leaves	Lemon wedges

1. Wash fish in cold water; drain; pat dry with paper towels. Scrub mussels and clams with brush or plastic scrubber. Wash shrimp and scallops in cold water; drain.

2. Preheat oven to 375°F. Tear off 6 (12-inch) squares of foil.

3. Place a fish diagonally on half of each square, 1½ inches from edges. Arrange 2 mussels, 2 clams, 2 shrimp, and 2 scallops on each fish.

4. Sprinkle each with ¼ teaspoon thyme, ¼ teaspoon marjoram, a sliver of garlic, ¼ teaspoon salt, dash pepper, ½ teaspoon olive oil, and 1½ teaspoons lemon juice.

5. Fold foil in diagonal; fold edges over twice, to seal securely.

6. Place foil packages on large cookie sheet or jelly-roll pan. Bake 25 to 30 minutes, or until clams and mussels open and fish is cooked through.

7. To serve: Slash a cross in each package; fold back corners. Garnish with lemon wedges. Or serve in individual shell dishes.

Makes 6 servings.

POULTRY

Pollame

Italians have a variety of unusual and good ways of cooking chicken. Chicken is considered more of a luxury meat in Italy than it is here, where modern methods of raising birds have made it an inexpensive meat. Some turkey is eaten in Italy, as well as duck, pigeons, and small game birds. These chicken recipes, as is typical of many Italian poultry dishes, are suitable for either young or old birds.

Hunter's Style Chicken

POLLO ALLA CACCIATORA CON POLENTA

2 (2-pound size) ready-to-cook broiler-fryers, cut up	1 can (1 pound, 1 ounce) Italian tomatoes, undrained
3 tablespoons olive or salad oil	1½ teaspoons salt
2 tablespoons butter or margarine	½ teaspoon dried basil leaves
1½ cups sliced onion	¼ teaspoon pepper
1 clove garlic, crushed	½ cup red wine
2 tablespoons chopped parsley	Polenta, page 57

1. Wash chicken; pat dry with paper towels.

2. Heat oil and butter in Dutch oven. Add chicken, a few pieces at a time, and brown well on all sides. Remove as browned, and set aside.

3. Add onion and garlic to Dutch oven, and sauté until golden brown—about 5 minutes. Add parsley, tomatoes, salt, basil, and pepper; mix well, mashing tomatoes with fork.

4. Bring to boiling. Reduce heat and simmer, uncovered, 20 minutes.

5. Add browned chicken and the wine; simmer, covered, 45 to 50 minutes, or until chicken is tender.

6. Meanwhile, make Polenta.

7. To serve, spoon chicken and some of sauce over polenta. Pass rest of sauce. If desired, garnish with chopped parsley.

Makes 6 to 8 servings.

Chicken Mantua Style

POLLO ALLA MANTOVANA

This dish is usually served with Saffron Rice.

4-pound ready-to-cook roasting chicken	2 tablespoons chopped parsley
1 teaspoon salt	1 cup tomato juice
¼ teaspoon pepper	1 chicken-bouillon cube, crumbled
¼ cup butter or margarine	8 pitted green olives
½ cup chopped onion	4 pitted ripe olives
½ cup chopped celery	Parsley sprigs

1. Wash chicken; pat dry with paper towels. Sprinkle inside with salt and pepper. Tie legs together; bend wing tips under body.

2. Heat butter in Dutch oven. Add chicken, and cook over medium heat until nicely browned on all sides—about 30 minutes. With two spoons, carefully remove chicken.

3. In same pan, sauté onion, celery, and chopped parsley until onion is tender—about 5 minutes. Stir in tomato juice and bouillon cube.

4. Return chicken to pan. Simmer, covered, 1½ hours, or until chicken is tender.

5. Remove chicken to heated platter; keep warm.

6. Strain drippings into 2-cup measure; skim off fat. Return drippings to pan—there should be about 1 cup. Chop 4 green olives. Add with rest of olives. Bring to boiling; reduce heat, and simmer, uncovered, 5 minutes.

7. To serve: Spoon part of gravy over chicken. Garnish with parsley sprigs. Pass remaining gravy.

Makes 6 servings.

Venetian Chicken Casserole

CASSERUOLA DI POLLO ALLA VENEZIANA

4-pound roasting chicken,
   cut up
2 tablespoons butter or
   margarine
2 tablespoons olive or salad oil
1 large onion, sliced
1 large carrot, sliced
1 stalk celery, sliced
1 can (1 pound) Italian
   tomatoes, undrained

1 tablespoon dried basil leaves
1 tablespoon dried oregano leaves
1½ teaspoons salt
¼ teaspoon cinnamon
⅛ teaspoon black pepper
4 whole cloves
½ cup dry white wine
¼ pound fresh mushrooms,
   washed and sliced
1 tablespoon flour

1. Wash chicken; pat dry with paper towels.

2. Heat butter and oil in Dutch oven. Add chicken, a few pieces at a time, and brown well on all sides. Remove as browned, and set aside.

3. Add onion, carrot, and celery to Dutch oven, and sauté until golden— about 5 minutes. Add tomatoes, basil, oregano, salt, cinnamon, pepper, and cloves; mix well, mashing tomatoes with fork.

4. Bring to boiling; reduce heat, and simmer, uncovered, 10 minutes.

5. Add browned chicken and the wine; simmer, covered, for 50 to 60 minutes, or until chicken is tender. Add mushrooms; cook, uncovered, 10 minutes longer.

6. Remove chicken to a warm, deep dish. Dissolve flour in 2 tablespoons water; stir into sauce; bring to boiling, stirring until thickened. Pour over chicken.

Makes 6 servings.

Cornish Hens on a Spit, with Polenta

POLENTA CON UCCELLINI

4 (1-pound size) frozen Rock
   Cornish hens, thawed
1 tablespoon lemon juice
1 teaspoon salt
1½ teaspoons dried thyme leaves
1½ teaspoons dried basil leaves
8 juniper berries, crushed
⅛ teaspoon pepper

Basting Sauce
⅓ cup melted butter or margarine
3 tablespoons lemon juice
1 teaspoon salt
2 teaspoons dried thyme leaves

Polenta, page 57

1. Rub inside of each hen's body cavity with lemon juice.

2. Combine 1 teaspoon salt, 1½ teaspoons thyme, the basil, juniper berries, and pepper. Sprinkle mixture inside each cavity.

3. Make Basting Sauce: Combine all ingredients. Brush hens well with some of sauce.

4. Tie legs of hens together; bend wings under. Crisscross string around the birds, securing the legs and wings. Adjust hens on electric rotisserie spit, pressing them close together.

5. Roast 1 hour and 15 minutes, basting frequently with sauce and drippings. Serve on polenta.

Makes 4 servings.

Note: If cooking outdoors, adjust barbecue spit 5 inches above prepared coals.

Duckling with Anchovy and Sausage

ANITRA ALL'ACCIUGA CON SALSICCE

2 (4½- to 5-pound size) ready-to-cook ducklings	1 pound Italian sweet sausages
½ teaspoon salt	1 tablespoon chopped garlic
⅛ teaspoon pepper	2 teaspoons dried rosemary leaves
4 tablespoons butter or margarine, melted	2 teaspoons sage
2 tablespoons lemon juice	1 bay leaf
	1 can (2 ounces) anchovy fillets, drained and chopped
Sauce	1 lemon, cut in half
6 slices bacon	2 cups dry red wine
2 tablespoons butter or margarine	½ cup wine vinegar
	3 tablespoons flour

1. Preheat oven to 425°F.

2. Remove giblets from ducklings; rinse in cold water, and put aside for sauce. Wash ducklings well under running water; drain; dry with paper towels. Bring skin of neck over back; fasten with poultry pin.

3. Sprinkle inside of each duckling with ¼ teaspoon salt and dash pepper.

4. Truss each duckling: Close the cavity with poultry pins; lace with twine. Tie ends of legs together; bend wing tips under body.

5. Place ducklings, breast side up, on rack in shallow roasting pan. Brush with some of melted butter. Roast, uncovered, 20 minutes. Prick

skin with a fork; turn ducklings breast side down, and brush with more butter. Roast 20 minutes longer. Turn again; sprinkle with lemon juice. Reduce heat to 375°F, and roast 40 minutes.

6. Meanwhile, make Sauce: Cook bacon in large Dutch oven until crisp. Remove, and drain on paper towels. Pour off all except 4 tablespoons fat. Add 2 tablespoons butter. Brown sausages, giblets, and necks in hot fat mixture, turning to brown all sides. Stir in garlic, rosemary, sage, bay leaf, the crumbled bacon, half of anchovies, lemon halves; cook until garlic is golden. Add wine, vinegar, and 1 cup water; bring to a boil. Cover; reduce heat, and simmer 20 minutes.

7. Cut ducklings into quarters. Place in the Dutch oven; baste with some of sauce. Roast, covered, 20 minutes. Remove cover; baste with more sauce, and roast, uncovered, 10 minutes.

8. Remove duckling to heatproof serving platter; keep warm. Cut sausages in half; place on platter. Discard neck and giblets.

9. Pour liquid from Dutch oven into 1-quart measuring cup. Skim off fat with a large spoon. Place paper towels on broth to absorb remaining fat. If necessary, add water to broth to make 3 cups. Return to Dutch oven; bring to boiling.

10. Blend flour with ½ cup cold water smoothly. Pour into boiling sauce, stirring constantly. Cook, stirring, until mixture thickens and comes to a boil again. Add remaining chopped anchovies. Add salt and pepper, if desired.

11. Pour some of hot sauce over duckling and sausages. Pass rest in sauceboat. Garnish platter with lemon slices, if desired.

Makes 6 to 8 servings.

MEAT

Carne

Veal is the favorite meat of Italy, and is also the best and most flavorful meat. It is used in a variety of dishes—small pieces flavor risotto, tender little scallops are cooked with lemon or Marsala; it is served hot as a roast or cold with tuna sauce, and braised shanks are one of the most famous dishes of the northern provinces.

Italian veal is entirely milk-fed; consequently, it is much more tender than American veal. Beef, on the other hand, is not as good as ours, and it is not as popular. There are many recipes for beef stews and the smaller cuts of meat. But one of the best Italian recipes reflects the superior quality of Tuscan beef—Florentine steak is charcoal broiled and flavored with olive oil, fresh black pepper, and lemon juice. Veal and pork chops are also cooked this way very successfully. Lamb and kid are the favorite meats of the south of Italy. Variety meats—liver, sweetbreads, brains, and heart—are inexpensive and used in pasta sauces and risotto. They are an example of the Italian cook's talent for making do with small quantities of meat. As a rule, meat, or at least a large cut of meat, is not eaten every day.

Meat is served with vegetables, and fried or roasted potatoes, and a salad.

Roast Veal Florentine

ARROSTO DI VITELLO ALLA FIORENTINA

Florentine Stuffing	1 tablespoon grated Parmesan
1 package (10 ounces) frozen	cheese
chopped spinach	1 teaspoon salt
¼ cup butter or margarine	½ teaspoon dried oregano leaves
1 cup chopped onion	⅛ teaspoon pepper
1 clove garlic, crushed	
1½ cups soft white-bread	5- to 6-pound leg of veal, boned,
crumbs	not rolled and tied
1 tablespoon chopped parsley	4 slices bacon

1. Make Florentine Stuffing: Cook spinach as package label directs. Drain well.

2. In hot butter in large skillet, sauté onion and garlic until onion is tender—about 5 minutes. Remove from heat.

3. Add spinach, bread crumbs, parsley, Parmesan, salt, oregano, and pepper; stir until well combined.

4. Preheat oven to 325°F.

5. Wipe veal with damp paper towels. Place, skin side down, on board. If necessary, pound with mallet to about 1-inch thickness.

6. Place stuffing lengthwise down center of veal. Bring long sides of meat over stuffing, and overlap. Fasten with skewers, and lace with twine.

7. Place, laced side up, in shallow, open roasting pan. Arrange bacon over top. Insert meat thermometer in thickest part of veal; do not rest it in stuffing.

8. Roast, uncovered, about 2½ hours, or until thermometer registers 170°F.

9. Cool ½ hour; refrigerate, covered, 1 to 2 hours, or until serving.

10. To serve: Remove skewers and twine from roast. Cut crosswise into ¼-inch-thick slices.

Makes 8 servings.

Veal Parmigiana

SCALOPPINE DI VITELLO ALLA PARMIGIANA

1 pound thin veal scaloppine	Tomato Sauce, below
2 eggs, beaten	1 package (8 ounces) mozzarella
1 cup seasoned dry	cheese, sliced
bread crumbs	¼ cup grated Parmesan cheese
½ cup olive or salad oil	

1. Preheat the oven to 350°F.

2. Wipe veal with damp paper towels. Dip in egg, then in bread crumbs, coating lightly.

3. In a large skillet, heat about ¼ cup oil. Add veal slices, a few at a time, and cook until golden brown on each side—2 to 3 minutes for each side. Add more oil as needed.

4. Place veal in 10-by-6½-by-2-inch baking dish, to cover bottom in a single layer. Add half the Tomato Sauce and half the mozzarella and Parmesan cheeses. Repeat the layers, ending with Parmesan cheese.

5. Cover baking dish with foil. Bake 30 minutes, or until bubbly. Makes 4 to 6 servings.

Tomato Sauce for Veal Parmigiana	2 teaspoons sugar
2 tablespoons olive or	¾ teaspoon salt
salad oil	½ teaspoon dried oregano leaves
½ cup chopped onion	¼ teaspoon dried basil leaves
1 clove garlic, crushed	¼ teaspoon pepper
1 can (1 pound, 1 ounce)	
Italian tomatoes, undrained	

1. In hot oil in medium saucepan, sauté onion and garlic until golden brown—about 5 minutes. Add tomatoes, sugar, salt, oregano, basil, and pepper; mix well, mashing the tomatoes with a fork.

2. Bring to boiling; reduce heat; simmer, covered, 10 minutes.

Roman Veal Scaloppini

SCALOPPINE DI VITELLO ALLA ROMANA

8 tablespoons butter or margarine	⅔ cup dry white wine
¾ pound mushrooms, sliced	Salt
1 small onion, finely chopped	¼ teaspoon dried tarragon
1 clove garlic, peeled	leaves, crushed
3 cups coarsely chopped,	12 thin veal scallops
peeled fresh tomatoes	(1½ pounds)
(about 2 pounds)	⅛ teaspoon pepper
	Grated Parmesan cheese

1. In 5 tablespoons hot butter in skillet, sauté mushrooms until golden brown—about 5 minutes. Add onion and garlic, and cook about 5 minutes, or until onion is golden.

2. Add tomatoes, wine, ¾ teaspoon salt, and tarragon, stirring until well blended. Reduce heat; simmer, covered and stirring occasionally, 30 minutes.

3. Meanwhile, wipe veal with damp paper towels. Sprinkle with ½ teaspoon salt and the pepper.

4. Heat 3 tablespoons butter in another skillet. Add veal, a few pieces at a time, and cook until lightly browned on both sides—about 5 minutes. Remove and keep warm.

5. Return veal to skillet. Remove garlic from sauce. Pour sauce over veal; simmer, covered, 5 minutes. Sprinkle with Parmesan cheese.

Makes 6 servings.

Veal Piccata

PICCATA DI VITELLO AL LIMONE

A Roman-style dinner would begin with Noodles Alfredo, and go on to Veal Piccata, a mixed green salad with sliced fresh mushrooms (the prettiest white ones the market has), and pimientos, and end with Peaches in Marsala and coffee. Drink a dry white wine or a light red with this typical meal of the central provinces of Italy.

1 pound thin veal scaloppine	2 tablespoons butter
2 tablespoons flour	½ lemon
½ teaspoon salt	½ cup dry white wine
¼ teaspoon pepper	Parsley

1. Wipe veal scaloppine with damp paper towels. Combine flour, salt, and pepper. Use flour mixture to coat veal well.

2. Heat butter in a medium skillet until it sizzles. Add half of veal slices, and cook over high heat until well browned on both sides; remove. Repeat with remaining slices of veal.

3. Return all veal to skillet. Slice lemon and add, along with dry white wine, to veal. Cook over low heat, covered, for 5 minutes.

4. Arrange veal on serving platter. Garnish with parsley sprigs. Makes 4 servings.

Veal Cutlets Piedmont Style

COTOLETTE ALLA PIEMONTESE

1½ pounds very thin veal scallops (about 10)	3 tablespoons olive oil 3 tablespoons butter or
½ pound mozzarella cheese, thinly sliced	margarine
¼ pound salami, thinly sliced	**Sauce**
3 tablespoons finely chopped green onions	½ cup butter or margarine 1 can (2 ounces) anchovy fillets,
2 tablespoons finely chopped parsley	drained and chopped ⅛ teaspoon pepper
2 eggs, beaten	¼ cup lemon juice
1 cup packaged dry bread crumbs	2 tablespoons chopped parsley

1. On one half of each veal scallop, place several mozzarella cheese slices, salami slices, some green onions, and some parsley.

2. Fold other half of veal scallop over filled half; secure open end and sides with wooden picks.

3. Dip each scallop into eggs, then into crumbs, coating evenly.

4. Heat oil and butter in large, heavy skillet. Add veal scallops, a few at a time; sauté until nicely browned—about 5 minutes on each side.

5. Meanwhile, make Sauce: Into hot butter in small saucepan, stir anchovies and pepper; heat several minutes. Stir in lemon juice and parsley to blend well.

6. To serve: Remove wooden picks. Place veal on hot platter; pour sauce over. Garnish with more parsley, if desired.

Makes 6 servings.

Braised Shin of Veal

OSSO BUCO

Osso Buco is traditionally served with Risotto alla Milanese, one of the few exceptions to the Italian way of always serving the starch before the meat course.

6 (¾- to 1-pound size) veal shanks	1 can (8 ounces) tomato sauce
⅓ cup flour	1 cup dry white wine
1½ teaspoons salt	1 teaspoon dried basil leaves
¼ teaspoon pepper	½ teaspoon dried thyme leaves
½ cup olive or salad oil	1 bay leaf
1 cup coarsely chopped onion	¼ cup finely chopped celery
1 cup sliced pared carrot	2 tablespoons chopped parsley
1 clove garlic, crushed	1 teaspoon grated lemon peel

1. Wipe the veal shanks with damp towels. Combine the flour, salt, and pepper; rub into veal shanks, coating them well on all sides.

2. Slowly heat oil in Dutch oven. Add veal shanks, three at a time, and brown well on all sides—30 minutes in all. Remove as browned.

3. Add onion, carrot, and garlic to Dutch oven; sauté until onion is tender—about 5 minutes. Add tomato sauce, white wine, basil, thyme, bay leaf, and the browned veal.

4. Bring the mixture to boiling. Then reduce heat, and let simmer, covered, for 1¾ to 2 hours, or until the veal is tender.

5. Sprinkle with celery, parsley, and lemon peel. Simmer, covered, 5 minutes longer.

Makes 6 servings.

Cold Veal with Tuna Fish Sauce

VITELLO TONNATO

This savory combination of cold veal slices with tuna fish sauce is a favorite summer dish all over Italy. It makes a fine buffet supper dish. Serve it with an antipasto of marinated artichoke hearts and tomatoes, sliced pickled beets, potato salad, black olives, and quartered hard-cooked eggs with crusty bread and butter. It should be accompanied by Cauliflower Salad or a mixed greens salad, and more bread should be passed. Spumone makes an attractive party dessert, and the wine should be a dry white like Orvieto, or a light red or rosé.

4-pound boned leg of veal,
  rolled and tied
1 large carrot, pared and cut up
1 celery stalk, cut up
1 large parsley sprig

1 medium onion, peeled and stuck
  with 2 whole cloves
1 clove garlic, split
1 teaspoon salt
Tuna Sauce, below

1. Day before serving: In 8-quart kettle, combine all ingredients (except Tuna Sauce) with 3½ quarts water, and bring to boiling.

2. Reduce heat, and simmer the veal, covered, 1½ hours, or until the meat is tender.

3. Remove veal from stock. (If desired, run meat under broiler to brown top slightly.) Let cool; then refrigerate until well chilled.

4. Strain veal stock. Reserve for Tuna Sauce.

5. To serve: Slice veal thinly. Arrange the slices in a row in center of a shallow dish. Pour Tuna Sauce around the veal slices. If desired, garnish with anchovy fillets and capers.

Makes 12 servings.

Tuna Sauce for Vitello Tonnato
3 cans (7-ounce size) tuna,
  drained
3 cans (2-ounce size) anchovy
  fillets, undrained
2 cups sliced celery
½ cup sliced carrot

½ teaspoon dried rosemary leaves
¼ teaspoon salt
¼ teaspoon pepper
Dash cayenne
1 jar (3¼ ounces) capers, drained
Reserved veal stock

1. Combine tuna, anchovies, oil from anchovies, celery, carrot, rosemary, salt, pepper, cayenne, capers, and 1 cup veal stock.

2. Bring mixture to boiling; reduce heat; simmer, covered, 30 minutes.

3. Remove from heat; let cool. Turn into blender container, one half at a time, with 1 cup veal stock; blend, covered, a few seconds, or just until blended but not smooth.

4. Measure sauce; add enough veal stock to make 6½ cups. Refrigerate overnight. If sauce seems too thick, add a little more veal stock.

Sweetbreads in Rice Ring

ANIMELLE IN UMIDO CON RISOTTO

2 pairs sweetbreads (2 pounds)
2 tablespoons lemon juice
2 teaspoons salt
1 bay leaf
¼ cup butter or margarine

¼ pound mushrooms, sliced;
  or 1 can (3 ounces) sliced
  mushrooms, drained
1 cup thinly sliced celery
½ cup thinly sliced carrot

½ cup thinly sliced onion
4 parsley sprigs
1 can (10½ ounces) condensed
  chicken broth, undiluted
½ cup sherry
½ teaspoon dried thyme leaves
1 tablespoon flour

Rice Ring
4 cups hot cooked rice
1 package (10 ounces) frozen
  green peas, cooked as package
  label directs
2 tablespoons butter or
  margarine, melted

1. Soak sweetbreads in ice water 1 hour. Drain.

2. Bring 2 quarts water to boiling in large saucepan. Add sweetbreads, lemon juice, salt, and bay leaf; return to boiling. Reduce heat, and simmer, covered, 20 minutes.

3. Drain sweetbreads. Plunge into ice water to keep white and firm; let cool completely. Remove the outer membrane and any fat in folds of sweetbreads. Cut each sweetbread in half lengthwise. Pat dry with paper towels.

4. Preheat oven to 375°F.

5. In ¼ cup hot butter in a heavy 10-inch skillet with heat-resistant handle, sauté mushrooms, celery, carrot, onion, and parsley until tender— will take about 5 minutes. Top with the sweetbreads; add chicken broth, ¼ cup sherry, and the thyme.

6. Bake, uncovered and basting two or three times with pan juices, until sweetbreads are browned and glazed—about 45 minutes.

7. Meanwhile, make Rice Ring: Butter a 5-cup ring mold. In large bowl, toss rice, peas, and melted butter until well combined. Pack lightly into prepared mold, smoothing top. Bake in oven with sweetbreads about 10 minutes, or until heated.

8. Run small spatula around edge of mold; invert on warm serving platter. Remove mold. With slotted utensil, remove sweetbreads and vegetables from pan, and arrange in center of rice ring. Keep warm.

9. Mix remaining sherry with flour; stir into pan drippings. Bring to boiling, stirring constantly; boil gently 2 minutes. Pour some of the sauce over the sweetbreads; pass remaining sauce.

Makes 4 to 6 servings.

Leg of Lamb with Anchovy Sauce

ABBACCHIO AL FORNO CON SALSA D'ALICI

6-pound leg of lamb
2 cloves garlic
1½ teaspoons salt

1 teaspoon ginger
1 teaspoon dried rosemary
  leaves

| ¼ teaspoon pepper | Anchovy Sauce, below |
| 1 cup white wine | Roasted New Potatoes, page 91 |

1. Preheat oven to 325°F. Wipe lamb with damp paper towels. Make 6 slits in lamb; insert ⅓ clove garlic in each. Mix salt, ginger, rosemary, and pepper; rub over lamb.

2. Place roast, fat side up, on rack in a shallow roasting pan. Insert meat thermometer in thickest part of meat, away from bone.

3. Roast, uncovered, 1 hour. Baste with ⅓ cup wine; roast, basting several times with wine, 1½ hours, or to 175°F. on thermometer.

4. Baste well with pan juices. Remove to serving platter; let stand in warm place 20 minutes before carving. Save drippings. Make Anchovy Sauce.

5. Place Roasted New Potatoes around lamb. Pass Anchovy Sauce. Makes 9 to 10 servings.

| **Anchovy Sauce for Lamb** | 2 tablespoons chopped parsley |
| 6 anchovy fillets, chopped | ½ teaspoon grated lemon peel |

1. Pour pan drippings from leg of lamb into 1-cup measure; skim off excess fat. Add water to make 1 cup; return to roasting pan.

2. Add anchovy fillets, and cook over medium heat, stirring, until mixture is well blended—about 2 minutes.

3. Add parsley and lemon peel; simmer 1 minute.

Steak with Tomato Sauce

BISTECCA ALLA PIZZAIOLA

A meal built around this recipe, suitable for entertaining, might begin with Stuffed Clams Oregano, and go on to Noodles Alfredo. The steak should be accompanied by Green Beans with Prosciutto. Dessert is Zabaglione with either fresh strawberries or fresh sliced peaches. Espresso coffee should end the meal, and the wine is Chianti.

2 tablespoons olive or salad oil	½ clove garlic, crushed
1 clove garlic, crushed	1 can (1 pound, 1 ounce) Italian
⅛ teaspoon pepper	plum tomatoes, undrained
4- to 4½-pound sirloin steak,	Finely chopped parsley
1½ inches thick	1 teaspoon salt
	1 teaspoon dried oregano leaves
Tomato Sauce	Dash pepper
1 tablespoon olive or salad oil	
½ cup sliced onion	

1. In large, shallow baking dish, combine 2 tablespoons oil; 1 clove garlic, and ⅛ teaspoon pepper.

2. Wipe steak with damp paper towels; rub oil mixture into both sides. Let steak stand in baking dish, covered, at room temperature 1 hour.

3. Meanwhile, make Tomato Sauce: In 1 tablespoon hot oil in medium saucepan, sauté onion (separated into rings), and ½ clove garlic until golden—about 5 minutes.

4. Add tomatoes, crushing whole tomatoes with fork. Add 1 tablespoon parsley, the salt, oregano, and dash pepper; blend well. Bring to boiling; reduce heat, and simmer, uncovered and stirring occasionally, 10 minutes. Keep warm.

5. Trim a little fat from steak; use to rub on broiler rack.

6. Broil steak, 5 inches from heat, 14 to 16 minutes per side for rare; 16 to 18 minutes per side for medium; 18 to 20 minutes per side for well done.

7. Remove steak to heated serving platter. Top with sauce and more chopped parsley.

Makes 6 to 8 servings.

Florentine Chuck Steak

BISTECCA ALLA FIORENTINA

4½- to 5-pound round-bone chuck steak, about 2 inches thick	¼ cup lemon juice
	½ teaspoon salt
	½ teaspoon coarsely ground black pepper
Instant meat tenderizer	
¼ cup olive or salad oil	

1. Wipe steak with damp paper towels. Sprinkle with meat tenderizer, as the label directs. Combine the oil, lemon juice, salt, and black pepper, and mix well.

2. Place steak on rack in broiler pan; brush with about 2 tablespoons oil mixture. Broil, 5 inches from heat, 20 minutes. Turn steak, and brush with more of the oil mixture. Broil steak 20 minutes longer for rare.

3. To serve: Slice thinly. Drizzle with any remaining oil mixture. Garnish with lemon wedges, if desired.

Makes 8 to 10 servings.

Italian Pork Chops Marsala

COSTOLETTE DI MAIALE ALLA MARSALA

Marinade	Dash cinnamon
¾ cup Marsala	Dash pepper
1½ tablespoons grated	
orange peel	6 loin pork chops, about 1 inch
¼ cup orange juice	thick (2¼ pounds)
1 clove garlic, crushed	2 tablespoons salad or olive oil
1 teaspoon salt	
½ teaspoon dried rosemary leaves	Glazed Orange Slices, below
Dash ground cloves	

1. Make Marinade: In small bowl, combine all marinade ingredients.

2. Wipe pork chops with damp paper towels. Trim off fat, if necessary. Place chops in shallow dish; pour marinade over all. Let stand 1 hour, turning chops at least once.

3. Drain marinade from chops; reserve. In hot oil in Dutch oven, brown chops well on both sides—about 15 minutes in all.

4. Pour reserved marinade over chops; simmer, covered, 45 to 50 minutes, or until tender.

5. Meanwhile, make Glazed Orange Slices.

6. Arrange pork chops on serving platter. Garnish with Glazed Orange Slices. Keep warm.

7. Heat drippings in Dutch oven to boiling; boil 1 minute. Strain, and pour over pork chops. Garnish with parsley, if desired.

Makes 6 servings.

Glazed Orange Slices	½ cup brown sugar, firmly packed
3 medium oranges	2 tablespoons light corn syrup
¼ cup butter or margarine	

1. Trim and discard ends from oranges.

2. Cut unpeeled oranges crosswise into slices, about ½ inch thick.

3. In large skillet, combine butter, sugar, and corn syrup; cook over medium heat, stirring, until sugar is melted and mixture boils.

4. Layer orange slices in skillet; cook, uncovered, 5 minutes. Turn slices, and cook 5 minutes longer, or just until orange slices are shiny and glazed.

Makes 6 servings.

Pork Chops Neapolitan

COSTOLETTE DI MAIALE ALLA NAPOLETANA

6 loin pork chops, ¾ inch thick (about 2 pounds)	½ teaspoon dried oregano leaves
2 tablespoons olive or salad oil	½ teaspoon dried basil leaves
1 cup chopped onion	⅛ teaspoon pepper
1 clove garlic, crushed	1 large green pepper, cut into 6 wedges
1 can (1 pound, 1 ounce) Italian tomatoes, undrained	1 can (4 ounces) button mushrooms, drained
1 teaspoon salt	

1. Wipe chops with damp paper towels.
2. In hot oil in large skillet, brown chops well on both sides. Remove from skillet.
3. Drain all but 1 tablespoon drippings from skillet. Add onion and garlic; sauté until onion is tender—about 5 minutes. Add tomatoes, salt, oregano, basil, and pepper; mix well, mashing tomatoes with fork.
4. Place pork chops in skillet. Arrange green pepper wedges, spoke fashion, between chops. Simmer, covered, 1¼ hours, or until chops are tender. Add mushrooms, and simmer 5 minutes longer.

Makes 6 servings.

Calf's Liver Veneziano

FEGATO ALLA VENEZIANA

1½ pounds calf's liver, sliced 1 inch thick	¼ cup olive or salad oil
¼ cup flour	2 pounds onions, thinly sliced
1½ teaspoons salt	½ teaspoon dried sage leaves
¼ teaspoon pepper	¼ cup dry white wine
¼ cup butter or margarine	1 tablespoon lemon juice
	2 tablespoons chopped parsley

1. With paper towels, pat liver dry. Cut into strips ⅛ inch wide (see Note).
2. On sheet of waxed paper, combine flour, salt, and pepper. Roll liver in mixture, coating well.
3. In large skillet, heat butter and 2 tablespoons oil. Sauté liver strips, turning frequently, until lightly browned on all sides—about 5 minutes. Remove, and set aside.
4. Add remaining oil to skillet. Sauté onion slices, stirring frequently,

until golden—about 10 minutes. Add sage. Cook, covered, over low heat 5 minutes.

5. Combine liver with onion, tossing lightly. Cook, covered, over low heat 5 minutes. Remove liver and onion to serving dish.

6. To drippings in skillet, add white wine and lemon juice; bring to boiling, stirring. Pour over liver and onion. Sprinkle with chopped parsley.

Makes 6 to 8 servings.

Note: To make liver easier to slice thinly, place in freezer long enough to chill thoroughly.

Hot and Sweet Sausages in Tomato Sauce, with Spaghetti

SALSICCIA ALLA ROMAGNOLA

For entertaining family style, this savory sausage and spaghetti recipe is perfect. The meal should begin with an antipasto platter of attractively arranged roasted sweet red peppers, a can of solid-pack tuna fish, marinated artichoke hearts, and slices of Provolone cheese. Bread sticks or grissini and butter are served with the antipasto. Buttered Italian green beans accompany the sausages and spaghetti. The dessert is Biscuit Tortoni, and the meal ends with espresso. The suitable wine is Chianti.

1 teaspoon olive or salad oil	2 packages (1-pound, 1⅔-ounce
1 large onion	size) spaghetti dinner with
8 sweet Italian sausages	mushroom sauce
(1½ pounds)	1 can (6 ounces) whole
4 hot Italian sausages	mushrooms, undrained
(¾ pound)	½ teaspoon oregano

1. Slowly heat a large, heavy skillet, lightly greased with oil. Peel onion and slice into rings. In hot skillet, sauté onion rings and sausages about 20 minutes; stir occasionally.

2. To boiling water, add spaghetti from both packages, a small amount at a time (so water will not stop boiling). Boil 8 to 10 minutes, or until of desired doneness. Drain in colander.

3. To sausages in skillet, add sauce from both packages of spaghetti, canned mushrooms with their liquid, and oregano; mix well. Bring to boiling; reduce heat, and simmer, covered, 5 minutes, or until serving.

4. To serve: Place spaghetti on serving platter. Top with sausages and mushroom sauce. Sprinkle with cheese from spaghetti package.

Makes 4 servings.

Vegetables

The soil of Italy seems particularly suited to growing vegetables. Their brilliant colors and plump shapes dominate the market stalls. They are grown everywhere, from window pots of basil and tomatoes to artichokes between rows of vines. Vegetables appear on the table at every meal, even breakfast, for crusty bread drizzled with olive oil and sliced tomatoes sprinkled with fresh herbs is offered for the first meal of the day in the southern provinces. Tables are set with platters of celery, small tomatoes, peppers, and anise-flavored fennel for guests to begin on before a pre-pared antipasto selection is brought on. Vegetables, either in salads or stuffed, often are the antipasto course, or they are served as a course by themselves. The simply cooked vegetables accompany the meat course and are known as contorno; more elaborate vegetable recipes can be the main course of a light meal.

Vegetables in Italy are very fresh—they come almost directly from the fields. Italian cooks choose their vegetables for perfection and small size, for they feel the most delicately flavored vegetable is the youngest one. Among the favorite vegetables are fennel, or finocchio, which is hard to find in this country, slender green zucchini and other summer squash, red and green sweet peppers, globe artichokes, fresh and dried mush-rooms, spinach, broccoli, and its cousin, broccoletti di rabe.

We are accustomed to steaming most of our vegetables and serving them plain. Italians prefer them flavored with olive oil or butter, garlic and herbs, or stewed in a combination of vegetables and tastes. For instance, spinach is briefly sautéed in a pan with butter, then a lemon is squeezed over it just before serving, or zucchini or eggplant are stewed with tomatoes.

Artichokes with Lemon Sauce

CARCIOFI AL LIMONE

¼ cup olive or salad oil
6 lemon slices
2 bay leaves
1 clove garlic, split
1 teaspoon salt
⅛ teaspoon pepper

4 large artichokes
  (about 3 pounds)

Lemon Sauce
¼ cup melted butter
2 tablespoons olive oil
2 tablespoons lemon juice

1. In large kettle, combine 3 quarts water with ¼ cup olive oil, lemon slices, bay leaves, garlic, salt, and pepper; bring to boiling.

2. Meanwhile, trim stalk from base of artichokes; cut a 1-inch slice from tops. Remove discolored leaves; snip off spike ends.

3. Wash the artichokes in cold water; drain.

4. Add to boiling mixture. Reduce heat; simmer, covered, 40 to 45 minutes, or until artichoke bases feel soft. Drain artichokes well.

5. Meanwhile, make Lemon Sauce: In a small bowl, mix the butter, olive oil, and lemon juice until well combined.

6. To serve: Place an artichoke and small cup of sauce on individual plates. To eat, pull out leaves, one at a time, and dip in sauce. Discard prickly choke.

Makes 4 servings.

Artichokes with Fresh Tomato Sauce

CARCIOFI ALLA SALSA DI POMODORO

3 tablespoons lemon juice
1½ teaspoons salt
4 large artichokes

Sauce
3 medium tomatoes
  (about 1 pound)

¼ cup butter or margarine
1 cup chopped onion
2 tablespoons flour
1½ teaspoons salt
¼ teaspoon dried thyme leaves
⅔ cup sauterne

1. In a large kettle, bring 3 quarts water, lemon juice, and 1½ teaspoons salt to boiling.

2. Meanwhile, wash artichokes. Trim stalks from base of artichokes; cut a 1-inch slice from top. Remove discolored and tough outer leaves; snip off spike ends of leaves. Cut in quarters and remove chokes.

3. Add artichokes to the boiling water; return to boiling. Boil gently, covered, about 20 minutes, or until bases of artichokes are tender. Drain.

4. Preheat oven to 400°F.

5. Make Sauce: Wash tomatoes, and remove stem ends. Cut into ½-inch cubes and set aside.

6. In hot butter in skillet, sauté onion until tender—about 5 minutes. Remove from heat; stir in flour, salt, thyme, and tomatoes until well blended. Gradually add ⅔ cup water and sauterne.

7. Bring to boiling, stirring constantly. Reduce heat, and simmer 3 minutes. Keep warm.

8. Place drained artichokes in a 9-by-9-by-2-inch or shallow oval baking dish. Add half the sauce.

9. Bake, uncovered, 10 minutes. When serving, pass remaining sauce. Makes 4 to 6 servings.

Artichokes with Lamb Stuffing

CARCIOFI RIPIENI DI ABBACCHIO

Stuffing	¼ teaspoon pepper
1½ pounds ground lamb	4 large artichokes*
½ cup packaged herb-	(about 3 pounds)
seasoned stuffing mix	
½ cup finely chopped onion	Sauce
1 egg	½ cup fresh lemon juice
¼ cup milk	¼ cup salad oil
2 tablespoons Worcestershire	1 clove garlic, crushed
sauce	¾ teaspoon salt
1 teaspoon salt	⅛ teaspoon pepper
½ teaspoon dried thyme leaves	
½ teaspoon dry mustard	Finely chopped parsley

1. Preheat oven to 350°F.

2. Make Stuffing: In lightly greased 1½-quart casserole, lightly toss all stuffing ingredients. Bake, covered, 1 hour, stirring occasionally.

3. Meanwhile, cook artichokes. Drain; cool slightly.

4. Remove choke and purplish inner leaves from center of each artichoke. Fill centers with some of stuffing mixture.

Cook according to Directions 1 through 4 for Artichokes with Lemon Sauce, page 83.

5. Loosen outer leaves halfway down side. Place remaining stuffing inside outer leaves. Arrange artichokes in large, shallow baking dish.

6. Make Sauce: Combine all sauce ingredients in jar with tight-fitting lid; shake vigorously to combine.

7. Sprinkle 1 tablespoon sauce over each artichoke; pour rest around artichokes.

8. Cover dish with foil; bake 15 minutes.

9. Lift artichokes to serving platter; sprinkle with parsley. Pour sauce into individual cups for dipping.

Makes 4 servings.

Artichoke Bottoms Florentine

CARCIOFI ALLA FIORENTINA

These make a nice garnish for a roast of lamb or veal.

1 can (15 ounces) artichoke bottoms, undrained	1 package (10 ounces) frozen creamed spinach

1. In small saucepan, heat artichoke bottoms in liquid from can.

2. Heat frozen spinach as package label directs.

3. Drain artichoke bottoms. Arrange around lamb on serving platter. Spoon spinach into artichokes.

Makes 6 servings.

Broccoli with Lemon Sauce

BROCCOLI AL LIMONE

1 bunch broccoli (about 1½ pounds) Salt	¼ cup olive oil ½ clove garlic, finely chopped 2 tablespoons lemon juice

1. Remove large leaves and tough portions of broccoli. Wash thoroughly; drain. Separate, splitting large stalks into quarters.

2. Place in a 6-quart saucepan; add 6 cups boiling water and 1 teaspoon salt. Cook, covered, 10 minutes, or until tender. Drain in colander.

3. In same pan, place olive oil and garlic; heat until bubbly. Add broccoli; sprinkle with lemon juice and ½ teaspoon salt. Cook, covered, 1 minute, or until broccoli is heated through. Serve hot.

Makes 4 servings.

Braised Carrots

STUFATINO DI CAROTE

1½ pounds carrots
1½ teaspoons salt
3 tablespoons butter or
   margarine

1 teaspoon sugar
⅛ teaspoon pepper
1 tablespoon chopped parsley

1. Pare carrots. Cut lengthwise into thin slices, then into julienne strips.
2. In medium saucepan, cook carrots and 1 teaspoon salt in boiling water to cover, covered, 10 to 15 minutes, or until tender. Drain well.
3. Add butter, sugar, ½ teaspoon salt, and the pepper. Heat over low heat, gently stirring occasionally, 5 to 6 minutes, or until the carrots are glazed.
4. Turn into serving bowl. Sprinkle with parsley.
Makes 6 servings.

Baked Stuffed Eggplant

MELANZANE RIPIENE

This recipe can be served as a hot antipasto or as the main dish for lunch or supper.

3 medium eggplants
   (about 3 pounds)
1½ teaspoons salt
Boiling water

Filling
¼ cup butter or margarine
1 cup chopped onion
2 cups chopped, peeled tomatoes
2 teaspoons salt
¼ teaspoon pepper
1 teaspoon dried basil leaves

½ teaspoon dried oregano leaves
½ cup packaged dry bread crumbs
2 cups chopped cooked ham

½ cup packaged dry bread crumbs
¼ teaspoon dried oregano leaves
¼ cup melted butter or
   margarine
6 mozzarella cheese slices,
   halved diagonally
12 anchovy fillets
Chopped parsley

1. Wash eggplants; halve lengthwise. Cut several deep gashes on cut side of each half, being careful not to cut through the skin.
2. Sprinkle cut sides with 1½ teaspoons salt. Let stand 30 minutes.
3. Preheat oven to 375°F.
4. Drain eggplant. Pat dry with paper towels.
5. Place eggplant halves, cut side down, in large roasting pan; add 1 cup

boiling water. Bake, uncovered, 15 minutes, or until just tender but not mushy.

6. Cool eggplant on wire rack. Scoop out pulp, leaving shells ¼ inch thick. Chop pulp coarsely; drain. Set pulp and shells aside.

7. Make Filling: In ¼ cup hot butter in large skillet, sauté onion until golden—about 5 minutes.

8. Add tomatoes, 2 teaspoons salt, the pepper, basil, ½ teaspoon oregano, ½ cup bread crumbs, the ham, and chopped eggplant; simmer, covered, 5 minutes.

9. Fill eggplant shells with filling, mounding it. Place in a shallow baking pan.

10. Toss ½ cup bread crumbs with ¼ teaspoon oregano and ¼ cup melted butter; sprinkle over filling. Arrange 2 cheese slices and 2 anchovy fillets over each eggplant half.

11. Bake about 15 minutes, or just until cheese melts and filling is heated through. Sprinkle with chopped parsley.

Makes 6 servings.

Eggplant Parmesan

MELANZANE ALLA PARMIGIANA

This is a typical Italian provincial dish and is a perfect luncheon dish.

Tomato Sauce	1 large eggplant
1½ tablespoons olive or	(about 1½ pounds)
salad oil	2 eggs, beaten
3 tablespoons finely chopped	1¼ cups packaged seasoned
onion	dry bread crumbs
3 cans (8-ounce size)	1 cup olive or salad oil
tomato sauce	½ pound mozzarella cheese,
1½ teaspoons dried oregano	sliced
leaves	2 tablespoons grated
½ teaspoon dried basil leaves	Parmesan cheese
¾ teaspoon salt	

1. Make Tomato Sauce: In hot oil in small saucepan sauté onion until golden—3 minutes. Add tomato sauce, oregano, basil, and salt; simmer 5 minutes. Set aside.

2. Preheat oven to 400°F.

3. Pare eggplant; cut crosswise into ¼-inch-thick slices. Dip into eggs, then into bread crumbs, coating completely.

4. Meanwhile, slowly heat ½ cup oil in large skillet. Sauté eggplant slices, a few at a time, until golden brown—about 3 minutes on each side. Add more oil as needed. Drain eggplant slices well on paper towels.

5. In a 12-by-8-by-2-inch baking dish, layer half of eggplant slices; top with half of Tomato Sauce and half of mozzarella cheese slices; repeat. Sprinkle top with Parmesan cheese.

6. Bake, uncovered, 15 to 20 minutes, or until cheese is melted and sauce is bubbly.

Makes 6 to 8 servings.

Eggplant-Parmesan Fritters

FRITTELLE DI MELANZANE PARMIGIANA

Fritto misto, a favorite Italian dish, is basically this recipe with the addition of artichoke hearts, cauliflower flowerets, and zucchini.

Salad oil or shortening for deep-frying	¾ cup grated Parmesan cheese
	1 egg white
	2 egg yolks
Batter	1½ tablespoons salad oil
¾ cup sifted all-purpose flour	¾ cup milk
2¼ teaspoons double-acting baking powder	
¾ teaspoon salt	1 eggplant (about 1½ pounds)

1. In electric skillet or deep-fat fryer, slowly heat oil (at least 1½ inches) to 375°F. on deep-frying thermometer.

2. Make Batter: Sift flour with baking powder and salt. Add cheese.

3. In small bowl, with rotary beater, beat egg white until stiff; set aside. With same beater, beat egg yolks with salad oil and milk. Gradually beat in flour mixture until smooth. Fold in egg white.

4. Wash eggplant well. Cut crosswise into ¼-inch-thick slices; cut very large ones in half crosswise.

5. Dip eggplant slices into batter, a few at a time; shake off excess batter. Deep-fry (fry only enough at one time to fit easily into skillet) 2 minutes on each side, or until tender and browned all over.

6. Lift from fat with slotted spoon; drain on paper towels. Keep warm while frying rest.

7. Serve 2 or 3 slices for a serving.

Makes 6 servings.

Green Beans Alfredo

FAGIOLINI ALL'ALFREDO

Italian green beans are wider and flatter than regular green, or string, beans.

1 package (9 ounces) frozen Italian green beans in butter sauce	¼ cup grated Parmesan cheese ⅛ teaspoon dried oregano leaves

1. Cook beans as package label directs.

2. Turn beans and sauce into serving dish. Sprinkle with cheese and oregano.

Makes 3 servings.

Green Beans with Prosciutto

FAGIOLINI CON PROSCIUTTO ALLA ROMANA

2 packages (9-ounce size) frozen Italian green beans	½ teaspoon salt
3 tablespoons butter or margarine	¼ teaspoon dried oregano leaves Dash pepper 2 slices prosciutto, cut into strips

1. Cook beans, following package label directions. Drain well.

2. Melt butter in medium saucepan. Add beans, salt, oregano, pepper, and prosciutto.

3. Cook over medium heat, stirring gently, just until heated through.

Makes 4 to 6 servings.

Sautéed Mushrooms

FUNGHI FRITTI

18 large mushrooms (1¼ pounds) ¼ cup butter or margarine	1 teaspoon dried marjoram leaves ½ teaspoon salt

1. Wash mushrooms; trim ends of stems.

2. Melt butter in large skillet. Add mushrooms; sprinkle with marjoram and salt.

3. Sauté mushrooms, turning frequently, 15 minutes, or until golden and tender.

Makes 6 servings.

Savory Stuffed Mushrooms

FUNGHI RIPIENI

16 medium-size mushrooms
(1 pound)
½ cup butter or margarine
¼ cup finely chopped
green pepper
¼ cup finely chopped onion

1½ cups fresh white-bread
cubes (¼ inch)
½ teaspoon salt
⅛ teaspoon pepper
Dash cayenne

1. Preheat oven to 350°F.
2. Wipe mushrooms with damp cloth. Remove stems, and chop stems fine; set aside.
3. Heat 3 tablespoons butter in large skillet. Sauté mushroom caps, on rounded side only, 2 to 3 minutes. Arrange, rounded side down, in shallow baking dish.
4. Heat rest of butter in same skillet. Sauté mushroom stems, green pepper, and onion until tender—about 5 minutes.
5. Remove from heat. Add bread cubes, salt, pepper, and cayenne; mix well.
6. Use mixture to fill mushroom caps, mounding in center; press filling down lightly.
7. Bake mushrooms 15 minutes. Then run under broiler about 2 minutes, just to brown tops.

Makes 8 servings.

Peppers and Zucchini Sauté

PEPERONI E ZUCCHINI SALTATI

3 slices bacon, cut in
1-inch pieces
½ cup sliced onion
2 red peppers, cut into strips
1 green pepper, cut into strips

1 medium zucchini, cut into
½-inch-thick slices (½ pound)
½ teaspoon salt
¼ teaspoon dried thyme leaves
Dash pepper

1. In large skillet, sauté bacon until crisp. Remove bacon bits, and set aside. In hot drippings, sauté onion until tender—will take about 5 minutes.
2. Add pepper strips and zucchini; sprinkle with salt, thyme, and pepper. Cook over medium heat, covered, 15 minutes, or just until vegetables are tender.

3. Turn into serving dish. Sprinkle with bacon.
Makes 4 to 6 servings.

Roasted New Potatoes

PATATE AL FORNO

2 pounds small new potatoes, pared	¼ cup butter or margarine
1 teaspoon salt	1 teaspoon seasoned salt

1. Cook potatoes in boiling water to cover with 1 teaspoon salt 10 minutes. Drain.

2. Melt butter in a 13-by-9-by-2-inch baking pan. Add potatoes, turning to coat with butter. Sprinkle with seasoned salt.

3. Bake, uncovered, in 325°F. oven, turning once, 40 minutes.
Makes 6 servings.

Baked Stuffed Onions

CIPOLLE RIPIENE AL FORNO

6 Bermuda onions (about 4 pounds)	1 teaspoon dried marjoram leaves
4 chicken-bouillon cubes	1 teaspoon salt
1 can (3 ounces) chopped mushrooms, drained	⅛ teaspoon pepper
4 slices bacon	3 tablespoons butter or margarine
1 cup soft bread crumbs	½ teaspoon paprika
2 tablespoons chopped parsley	

1. Peel onions; cut a thin slice from top of each. Place onions in large saucepan or small kettle; add bouillon cubes and 2 quarts water. Bring to boiling; reduce heat, and simmer until almost tender—30 to 35 minutes. Drain, and let cool.

2. Preheat oven to 400°F.

3. With small knife or teaspoon, remove centers of onions, leaving outside layers about ½ inch thick. Invert to drain.

4. Chop centers fine; measure 1 cup. Chop mushrooms fine.

5. Sauté bacon until crisp; crumble. Reserve bacon fat.

6. In medium bowl, combine crumbled bacon, chopped onion, mushrooms, bread crumbs, parsley, marjoram, salt, and pepper; toss with a fork to mix well. Mix in 2 tablespoons reserved bacon fat.

7. Melt butter in shallow baking dish; add paprika. Place onions in dish, brushing all over with butter mixture. Fill onions with stuffing; bake 20 minutes.

Makes 6 servings.

Broiled Tomato Halves

POMODORI ALLA GRIGLIA

6 small tomatoes (1½ pounds)	1 tablespoon
1 tablespoon butter or	seasoned salt
margarine	

1. Wash tomatoes; cut in half crosswise. Dot with butter; sprinkle with seasoned salt. Place in a 12-by-8-by-2-inch baking pan; refrigerate, covered.

2. At serving time, broil tomatoes, 4 inches from heat, 5 minutes, or until bubbly and heated through.

Makes 6 servings.

Sautéed Tomatoes

POMODORI SALTATI

2 large tomatoes	¼ teaspoon salt
2 tablespoons butter or	Dash pepper
margarine	1 teaspoon sugar
½ teaspoon dried basil leaves	

1. Wash tomatoes; cut out core and cut in quarters.

2. In medium skillet, melt butter over low heat. Add tomatoes; sprinkle with basil, salt, and pepper; sauté 5 minutes.

3. With slotted spatula, turn tomatoes. Sprinkle with sugar; sauté 3 minutes longer, or until cooked through.

4. Arrange as garnish on platter with meat.

Makes 4 servings.

Braised Fresh Spinach

STUFATINO DI SPINACI

3 pounds spinach	¼ teaspoon salt
¼ cup butter or margarine	Dash pepper
1 small whole onion	1 tablespoon lemon juice

1. Wash spinach well; remove and discard stems; break large leaves. Pat dry between paper towels.

2. Melt butter in large saucepan or kettle over medium heat. Add onion. Add spinach, a handful at a time, tossing with butter until wilted.

3. When all is added, reduce heat; simmer 4 or 5 minutes, stirring occasionally, or until the liquid has evaporated.

4. Remove from heat. Add salt, pepper, and lemon juice. Turn into heated serving dish. Remove and discard onion.

Makes 6 servings.

Spinach Ring with Sautéed Tomatoes

SFORMATO DI SPINACI E POMODORI

4 tablespoons butter or margarine	1 tablespoon grated Parmesan cheese
¼ cup chopped onion	
2 packages (10-ounce size) frozen chopped spinach	**Sautéed Tomatoes**
¾ cup light cream	2 tablespoons butter or margarine
4 eggs, slightly beaten	½ teaspoon salt
¾ cup milk	⅛ teaspoon dried oregano leaves
1 teaspoon salt	1 pint cherry tomatoes
¼ teaspoon garlic salt	

1. Preheat over to 325°F. Generously butter a 5½-cup ring mold.

2. In 4 tablespoons hot butter in large saucepan, sauté onion until tender—about 5 minutes.

3. Add spinach. Cook, covered and breaking up spinach with fork, about 5 minutes, or until thawed. Then cook, uncovered and stirring occasionally, until liquid has evaporated.

4. Stir in cream; simmer 2 minutes.

5. In medium bowl, beat eggs with milk, 1 teaspoon salt, and the garlic salt just until combined. Stir in spinach mixture and Parmesan.

6. Pour into prepared mold. Place in shallow pan; pour hot water to 1-inch depth around mold. Lay sheet of waxed paper over top of mold.

7. Bake 40 minutes, or until knife inserted in ring comes out clean.

8. Meanwhile, prepare Sautéed Tomatoes: Heat butter in medium skillet. Stir in salt and oregano. Add tomatoes, and cook over medium heat, stirring occasionally, until skins start to break—3 to 5 minutes. Keep warm.

9. To serve: Run small spatula around side and center of mold, to loosen. Invert onto heated serving plate. Spoon tomatoes into center.
Makes 6 servings.

Zucchini and Tomatoes

ZUCCHINI E POMODORI

6 small zucchini	1 tablespoon olive oil
2 tomatoes, peeled	Salt
and sliced thin	Pepper
¼ cup finely chopped onion	1 tablespoon grated
2 tablespoons chopped parsley	Parmesan cheese

1. Parboil zucchini until tender-crisp. Cut in ¼-inch slices.
2. Place in a shallow casserole in alternate layers with the tomatoes and onion. Sprinkle with parsley and olive oil. Season with salt and pepper. Sprinkle with cheese.
3. Bake at 325°F. for 10 to 15 minutes, or until vegetables are sizzling hot and cheese is brown.
Makes 6 servings.

Braised Zucchini and Onions

STUFATINO DI ZUCCHINI E CIPOLLE

2 teaspoons seasoned salt	2 pounds small white onions,
½ teaspoon dried basil leaves	peeled
Dash pepper	8 small zucchini (2 pounds), cut
1 beef-bouillon cube,	on diagonal into 1½-inch slices
crumbled	¼ cup butter or margarine

1. In 10-inch skillet with tight-fitting cover, bring to boiling 1½ cups water, the salt, basil, pepper, and bouillon cube.
2. Add onions; cook, covered, over medium heat, 15 minutes.
3. Layer zucchini on top of onions; cook, covered, 10 minutes, or just until vegetables are tender.
4. Drain. Return vegetables to skillet, and continue cooking, uncovered, a few minutes, to dry out vegetables.
5. Add butter; toss gently to coat vegetables.
Makes 10 servings.

Shrimp-stuffed Zucchini

ZUCCHINI RIPIENI DI SCAMPI

Cold Shrimp-stuffed Zucchini and hot Ham Hash in Zucchini Shells are both good antipasti.

4 medium zucchini	Pepper
3 tablespoons lemon juice	¼ cup grated Bel Paese cheese
1 cup coarsely chopped cooked shrimp	2 medium tomatoes, cut into wedges
3 tablespoons bottled Italian dressing	1 can (3⅞ ounces) pitted ripe olives, drained
⅛ teaspoon garlic powder	Italian dressing
Salt	

1. Scrub zucchini very well with vegetable brush. Place in large saucepan; add just enough cold water to cover.

2. Bring to boiling; reduce heat, and simmer, covered, 10 minutes, or until tender.

3. Drain zucchini; let cool. Cut in half lengthwise; scoop out and reserve centers. Brush cut sides of zucchini with the lemon juice.

4. Chop zucchini centers coarsely. In small bowl, combine chopped zucchini with shrimp, 3 tablespoons Italian dressing, the garlic powder, and salt and pepper to taste.

5. Fill zucchini with shrimp mixture. Sprinkle some of the grated cheese over each.

6. Refrigerate zucchini at least 1 hour before serving.

7. To serve: Place stuffed zucchini half on each of 8 chilled salad plates.

8. Arrange tomato wedges and olives around zucchini, for garnish. Pass more Italian dressing.

Makes 8 servings.

Ham Hash in Zucchini Shells

ZUCCHINI RIPIENI DI PROSCIUTTO

2 medium zucchini (about 1 pound)	**Ham Hash**
½ teaspoon salt	1 cup finely chopped cooked ham (4 ounces)

1 cup finely chopped
cooked potato
3 tablespoons mayonnaise or
cooked salad dressing
3 tablespoons finely chopped
green pepper

2 tablespoons finely chopped onion
Dash pepper

2 slices mozzarella cheese,
cut in strips

1. Wash zucchini well, **scrubbing** with vegetable brush. Halve lengthwise. In skillet, bring 1 inch water to boiling. Add salt. Place zucchini, cut side down, in water. Simmer, uncovered, 10 to 15 minutes, or until tender but not mushy. Drain.

2. Preheat oven to 350°F.

3. Meanwhile, make Ham Hash; In medium bowl, combine all ingredients for hash; mix until well blended.

4. Carefully scoop pulp from zucchini, leaving shells ¼ inch thick. Add pulp to hash. Fill zucchini shells with hash, mounding high. Cover with cheese strips. Place shells on cookie sheet.

5. Bake, uncovered, 15 minutes, or until cheese is melted, hash is hot. Makes 4 servings.

Desserts

Italians love sweets, but rich desserts are rarely served at home. Fruit and cheese, or fruit alone, end the typical Italian meal. Decorated cakes and molds or bombes of ice creams are usually bought rather than made at home and are served at parties and celebrations. A number of sweets, though, are made for holidays or feast days: Panettone, Milan's Christmas cake; Lombardy's Easter bread, colomba pasquale; Tuscany's castagnaccio alla fiorentina, a chestnut flour cake eaten at Lent; panforte, a fruitcake sold at Siena's medieval banner festival; and cassata alla Siciliana, a ricotta-filled cake served at Christmas and Easter. Christmas is the time for giving and enjoying the almond nougat, torrone, and the sweet cookies, amaretti and the pinocatte of Perugia.

Fruit is usually served at almost every meal. Italians can choose from melons, oranges, figs, peaches, plums, apricots, apples, pears, cherries, strawberries, and raspberries. Fruit is either eaten raw, peeled and then cut up with a knife and fork, or it is prepared simply. Strawberries are sprinkled with sugar and wine or orange juice. Peaches are soaked in Marsala, or several fruits are sliced and combined with a dash of liqueur.

Dessert cheeses are Gorgonzola, best with an apple or a pear and a glass of red wine; Bel Paese, probably Italy's favorite dessert cheese; cacciocavallo and stracchino, both good with plums and other firm fleshed fruits; and taleggio. Mascarpone is a rich triple-crème cheese that is too fragile to import, but French triple-crème cheeses that are very similar can be found here. Mascarpone, or a substitute, is delicate enough to pair with fresh strawberries and raspberries.

Ice cream is an Italian invention. There are rich fresh fruit ice creams, gelati; refreshing fruit or coffee water ices, granite; almond-flavored biscuit tortoni; spumone, a lavish combination of flavors and ice creams; and cassata, the northern Italian ice-cream bombes.

Cakes are luxuriously rich, beautifully decorated with whipped cream, chocolate curls, candied fruits, and nuts. They are truly party fare. Such well-known desserts as cassata alla Siciliana, spongecake layered with ricotta filling, zuppa inglese, tipsy cake, and cannoli, ricotta-filled pastry tubes, are time consuming to prepare but the results are delicious and satisfying.

Fresh Strawberries in Red Wine

FRAGOLE AL VINO ROSSO

2 pint boxes fresh strawberries   1 cup red wine
½ cup sugar

1. Gently wash strawberries in cold water; drain and hull.
2. In medium bowl, gently toss strawberries with sugar. Add wine.
3. Refrigerate at least 2 hours, stirring occasionally.
Makes 6 servings.

Peaches in Marsala

PESCHE AL MARSALA

Fresh peaches, peeled and sliced, nectarines, and plums, are also a good choice to combine with Marsala. Sugar the fruit to taste, then follow the recipe below.

1 can (1 pound, 14 ounces)   ½ cup cream Marsala
    peach halves   1-inch cinnamon stick

1. Drain the peach halves, reserving 1 tablespoon of the peach syrup.
2. In medium bowl, combine peaches, Marsala, cinnamon stick, and reserved syrup.
3. Refrigerate, covered, until the peaches are very well chilled—at least 2 hours.
4. To serve: Turn peaches and liquid into individual dessert dishes.
Makes 4 servings.

Fresh Peach Ice Cream

GELATO DI PESCHE

2 pounds fresh, ripe peaches	2 tablespoons confectioners' sugar
or nectarines	2 eggs yolks
3 tablespoons lemon juice	1 cup heavy cream
1½ cups granulated sugar	Few drops yellow food color
2 egg whites	(optional)

1. Peel peaches; halve; remove pits. In medium bowl, combine peaches with lemon juice; crush with potato masher. Stir in granulated sugar.

2. In small bowl of electric mixer, at high speed, beat egg whites with confectioners' sugar until soft peaks form. Turn into large bowl.

3. Using same beater, beat egg yolks until thick and lemon-colored.

4. Fold yolks gently into whites, using wire whisk or rubber scraper.

5. Whip cream until soft peaks form. Fold gently into egg mixture; add food color. Fold in peaches. Pour into 2 (1-quart) ice-cube trays.

6. Freeze until firm around the edges—about 1 hour.

7. Transfer to large bowl of electric mixer; beat, at high speed, just until smooth and creamy but not melted. Return to ice-cube trays; freeze until firm. Remove from freezer 15 minutes before serving.

Makes about 2 quarts; 8 servings.

Coffee Ice

GRANITA DI CAFFÈ

3 tablespoons instant	4 ice cubes
espresso coffee	Whipped cream
⅔ cup sugar	

1. In a 2-quart saucepan, combine the instant coffee, sugar, and 1 cup water. Bring to boiling, stirring constantly. Reduce heat, and simmer 5 minutes. Remove from heat.

2. Add 1 cup water and the 4 ice cubes; stir until ice is melted. Pour into refrigerator tray. Freeze until firm 1 inch from edge—will take about 1 hour and 45 minutes.

3. Turn into a large bowl. With electric mixer at medium speed, beat until mixture is smooth and no large ice crystals remain.

4. Turn into 2 refrigerator trays; freeze until almost solid—will take about 1 hour.

5. Stir ice. Spoon into chilled parfait glasses or sherbet dishes. Serve ice at once, topped with whipped cream.

Makes 4 servings.

Biscuit Tortoni

BISCOTTI TORTONI

3 egg whites	Almond extract
¾ cup sugar	1½ cups heavy cream
Dash salt	¾ teaspoon vanilla extract
¼ cup whole blanched almonds	12 candied cherries

1. In small bowl of electric mixer, let egg whites warm to room temperature—about 1 hour.

2. Combine ¼ cup water with the sugar in a 1-quart saucepan; cook over low heat, stirring, until sugar is dissolved.

3. Bring to boiling over medium heat; boil, uncovered and without stirring, to 236°F. on candy thermometer, or until syrup spins a 2-inch thread when dropped from a spoon.

4. Meanwhile, at high speed, beat egg whites with salt just until stiff peaks form when beater is slowly raised.

5. Pour hot syrup in thin stream over egg whites, beating constantly until mixture forms very stiff peaks when beater is raised. Refrigerate, covered, 30 minutes.

6. Meanwhile, preheat oven to 350°F. Place almonds in shallow pan and bake just until toasted—8 to 10 minutes. Finely grind almonds in a blender.

7. Turn into a small bowl. Blend in 1½ teaspoons almond extract. Set aside.

8. In medium bowl, beat cream with ¼ teaspoon almond extract and the vanilla until stiff. With wire whisk or rubber scraper, fold into egg-white mixture until thoroughly combined.

9. Spoon into 12 paper-lined 2½-inch muffin-pan cups. Sprinkle with almond mixture; top with a cherry.

10. Cover with foil; freeze until firm—several hours or overnight. Serve right from freezer.

Makes 12 servings.

Chocolate and Coffee Ice Cream Bombe
CASSATA DI CIOCCOLATA E CAFFÈ

3 pints chocolate ice cream	1 cup heavy cream
4 pints coffee ice cream	Chocolate curls

1. Place a 9-inch spring-form pan in freezer to chill before using—at least 20 minutes.

2. Remove 2 pints chocolate ice cream from freezer, and place in refrigerator to soften slightly—15 to 20 minutes.

3. Make ice-cream shell: With back of large spoon, quickly press softened chocolate ice cream to bottom and side of chilled pan. (If the ice cream softens too much while making shell, return pan and remaining ice cream to freezer just until firm enough to mold easily.)

4. Freeze shell until firm—at least 1 hour.

5. Soften remaining chocolate ice cream and the coffee ice cream in the refrigerator. Press coffee ice cream in center of firm shell, pressing down firmly. Top entire mold with chocolate ice cream, making it smooth with a broad spatula.

6. Quickly cover top with plastic film; then wrap with freezer-wrapping material. Seal; label; return to freezer.

7. Make frozen whipped-cream rosettes: Whip cream until stiff. Press through pastry bag, using number 6 decorating tip, onto cookie sheet or tray, to make 24 rosettes. Freeze until firm—about 2 hours. Then quickly remove to plastic bags. Label and return to freezer.

8. To serve: Remove from freezer as many rosettes as desired. Unmold bombe: Wipe outside of pan and clamp with hot, damp cloth; remove side of pan. With sharp knife dipped in hot water, cut desired number of servings. Rewrap remaining bombe and return to freezer.

9. Decorate each slice of bombe with a whipped-cream rosette and chocolate curls. (Or if serving whole bombe, arrange all whipped-cream rosettes on top.)

Makes 24 servings.

Della Robbia Ice Cream Wreath

CASSATA ALLA DELLA ROBBIA

4 pints vanilla ice cream
1 jar (9½ ounces) marrons
  in vanilla syrup
2 tablespoons brandy

1 package (8 ounces) marzipan
  fruits
½ cup assorted nuts (walnuts,
  Brazil nuts, pecans, filberts,
  almonds)

1. Place a 1½-quart ring mold in freezer, to chill well.

2. Press ice cream firmly and evenly into chilled mold. Freeze, covered, until very firm—several hours or overnight.

3. To unmold: Dip ring mold into warm water; invert onto serving plate or cookie sheet. Return ice cream to freezer until top is firm.

4. Drain marrons, reserving syrup. Set aside 4 marrons for decorating ice-cream ring. Chop remaining marrons, and add to reserved syrup, with brandy; refrigerate.

5. To decorate ice cream: Arrange marzipan fruits, the 4 marrons, and the nuts on top of firm ring. Return to freezer. If keeping more than one day, wrap with plastic film.

6. To serve: Garnish ice cream ring with small leaves, if desired, so that it resembles a wreath. Pass marron sauce.

Makes 10 servings.

Ice Cream Bombe

SPUMONI

This is an elegant and classic Italian dessert. It and the Della Robbia Ice Cream Wreath ought to bring out all of a cook's inventive flair for decorating. They should be very fancy and pretty desserts.

3 pints chocolate ice cream,
  slightly soft
1 pint pistachio ice cream,
  slightly soft
2 pints vanilla ice cream,
  slightly soft

½ cup candied mixed fruits
2 teaspoons rum or rum
  flavoring
1½ cups heavy cream, whipped

1. Place a 2½-quart melon mold in freezer.

2. In large bowl, with portable electric mixer, beat the chocolate ice cream until smooth but not melted. With spoon, quickly press evenly

inside the chilled melon mold to make a 1-inch-thick layer. Freeze until it is firm.

3. In medium bowl, beat the pistachio ice cream until smooth. Then press evenly over chocolate-ice-cream layer. Freeze until firm.

4. In large bowl, combine the vanilla ice cream, candied fruits, and rum; beat until well blended but not melted. Press into center of mold. Freeze until firm.

5. To unmold spumoni, let mold stand at room temperature 5 minutes. Invert over serving plate. Hold hot, damp dishcloth over mold, and shake to release. Return to freezer until surface is firm.

6. To decorate, spread three fourths of whipped cream over mold. Place remaining whipped cream in pastry bag with decorating tip, and pipe on mold decoratively. Return to freezer until serving time.

Makes 16 to 20 servings.

Marsala-flavored Custard

ZABAGLIONE

An attractive way of serving Zabaglione is to pour it over chilled, perfect, fresh strawberries. Zabaglione is also delicious as a cold dessert. When the custard holds its shape (see Direction 3), set top of the double boiler in a large bowl filled with cracked ice and continue beating until the Zabaglione is *completely cold*. It must be beaten until it is quite cold or it will collapse and separate. Pour it into dessert glasses and refrigerate until ready to serve. Cold Zabaglione is delectable combined with fresh strawberries or fresh peach slices.

6 egg yolks	⅓ cup Marsala
3 tablespoons sugar	

1. In top of double boiler, with portable electric mixer at high speed, or with rotary beater, beat the egg yolks with sugar until they are light and fluffy.

2. Gradually add Marsala, beating until well combined.

3. In top of double boiler, over hot, not boiling, water, beat at medium speed 8 minutes, or until mixture begins to hold its shape.

4. Turn into 4 dessert glasses. Serve at once, or while still slightly warm. (Zabaglione separates on standing.)

Makes 4 servings.

Glazed Green Grape Tart

TORTA D'UVA

Italians are fond of fresh-fruit tarts which are similar to the French fruit-and cream-filled tarts. In the Italian version 1 teaspoon of grated lemon rind is often added to the piecrust. The making of this dessert is detailed, but time is saved by using prepared piecrust and filling mixes.

1 package (9½ ounces)
   piecrust mix

Filling
1 package (3 ounces) vanilla-
   pudding-and-pie-filling mix
1½ cups milk

½ cup heavy cream

3 tablespoons Marsala or
   liqueur

1½ pounds (3 cups) seedless
   green grapes, washed, stems
   removed

Glaze
⅔ cup apple jelly

1. Make pastry: Prepare piecrust mix as package label directs. On lightly floured surface, roll out half to an 11-inch circle. Use to line a 9-inch pie plate. Trim overhang to ½ inch; make a stand-up edge; crimp edge decoratively. Prick pastry well all over with a fork. Refrigerate 30 minutes.

2. Make pastry leaves: Cut out of aluminum foil 5 patterns the shape of grape leaves about 6 inches long. On lightly floured surface, roll out remaining pastry to a square, about 12 inches. Place foil patterns on pastry; press on gently. With tip of sharp knife, cut around patterns. Lift each pastry leaf, with foil, and turn over. Prick leaves well all over with a fork. Drape leaves over edge of a second pie plate, foil side down. Refrigerate 30 minutes.

3. Preheat oven to 450°F.

4. Make Filling: Make pudding-and-pie-filling mix as package label directs for pudding, using 1½ cups milk. Remove from heat; cover top with plastic film. Refrigerate.

5. Bake pie shell and pastry leaves, still on pie plate, on a cookie sheet, 8 to 10 minutes, or until golden. Cool completely on wire racks. Remove foil from leaves.

6. In medium bowl, whip cream just until stiff. Fold Marsala into cooled filling; then fold in cream. Pour into cooled pie shell, spreading evenly. Place grapes on filling, to cover completely.

7. Make Glaze: In small saucepan over moderate heat, melt jelly with

1 tablespoon water; bring just to boiling. Cool slightly; then spoon over grapes, to glaze them. Refrigerate at least 1 hour.

8. To serve: Place pie in center of large serving tray. Arrange pastry leaves and, if desired, additional fresh grapes around pie.

Makes 8 servings.

Italian Cheese Pie

TORTA DI RICOTTA

Crust
1½ cups unsifted all-purpose
    flour
1¼ teaspoons baking powder
½ teaspoon salt
3 tablespoons butter or
    margarine, softened
¼ cup sugar
1 egg
½ teaspoon vanilla extract
½ teaspoon grated orange peel
1 tablespoon orange juice
    or whisky

1 egg, separated

Filling
1 container (15 ounces)
    ricotta cheese
¾ cup sugar
3 eggs
1½ teaspoons flour
1 teaspoon vanilla extract
½ teaspoon grated lemon peel

1. Make Crust: Sift flour with baking powder and salt. Set aside.

2. In medium bowl, with electric mixer, beat butter with sugar and 1 egg until light and fluffy. Beat in vanilla, orange peel, and orange juice.

3. Add half of flour mixture; with wooden spoon, beat until well blended. Add remaining flour mixture, mixing with hands until dough leaves side of bowl and holds together.

4. Turn out onto board; knead several times to blend well. Set aside, covered.

5. Make Filling: In a medium bowl, with portable electric mixer, beat ricotta cheese until it is creamy. Add sugar, eggs, flour, vanilla, and lemon peel; beat until well combined.

6. Preheat oven to 350°F.

7. Divide crust in half. Roll one half between 2 sheets of waxed paper to an 11-inch circle. Remove top paper. Fit crust into a 9-inch pie plate; trim to edge of plate. Brush with egg white.

8. Roll remaining crust to ⅛ inch thickness. With pastry cutter, cut into 10 strips, ½ inch wide.

9. Turn filling into lined pie plate. Place 5 pastry strips across filling,

pressing firmly to edge of pie plate. Place remaining strips across first ones, to make lattice.

10. Reroll trimmings, and cut into ½-inch-wide strips. Place around edge of pie, and with fork, press firmly to pie plate.

11. Beat egg yolk with 1 tablespoon water; brush over crust. Place a strip of foil, about 2 inches wide, around edge of crust, to prevent over-browning.

12. Bake about 50 minutes, or until top is golden brown and filling is set.

13. Cool on wire rack. Then refrigerate until well chilled—8 hours or overnight.

Makes 6 to 8 servings.

Sicilian Pastries

CANNOLI

Filling

3 pounds ricotta cheese
2½ cups confectioners' sugar
¼ cup semi-sweet-chocolate
  pieces or grated sweet
  chocolate
2 tablespoons chopped citron
10 candied cherries, finely
  chopped
½ teaspoon cinnamon

Cannoli Shells

3 cups sifted all-purpose flour
1 tablespoon sugar
¼ teaspoon cinnamon
¾ cup Port

Salad oil or shortening for
  deep-frying
1 egg yolk, slightly beaten

Chopped pistachio nuts (optional)
Confectioners' sugar

1. Make Filling: In a large bowl, with portable electric mixer, beat ricotta cheese 1 minute. Add 2½ cups confectioners' sugar, and beat until light and creamy—about 1 minute.

2. Add chocolate, citron, cherries, cinnamon; beat at low speed until well blended. Refrigerate, covered, until well chilled—at least 2 hours. Meanwhile, make Cannoli Shells.

3. Sift flour with sugar and cinnamon onto a board. Make a well in center, and fill with Port. With a fork, gradually blend flour into Port. When dough is stiff enough to handle, knead about 15 minutes, or until dough is smooth and stiff (if too moist and sticky, knead in a little more sifted flour).

4. Refrigerate dough, covered, 2 hours.

5. In deep-fat fryer, electric skillet, or heavy saucepan, slowly heat salad oil (3 to 4 inches deep), to 400°F on deep-frying thermometer.

6. Meanwhile, on lightly floured surface, roll one third of dough to paper thinness, making a 16-inch round. Cut into eight 5-inch circles. Wrap a circle loosely around a 6-inch-long cannoli form or dowel, 1 inch in diameter; seal with egg yolk.

7. Gently drop dough-covered forms, two at a time, into hot oil, and fry 1 minute, or until browned on all sides (turn, if necessary). With tongs or slotted utensil, lift out of oil, and drain on paper towels. Carefully remove forms. Continue until all dough is used.

8. Just before serving, with teaspoon or small spatula, fill shells with ricotta mixture. Garnish ends with chopped pistachios; sprinkle tops with confectioners' sugar.

Makes 24.

Note: Cannoli Shells can be made a day or two ahead and stored, covered, at room temperature, then filled about 1 hour before serving.

Tipsy Cake

ZUPPA INGLESE

Spongecake Layers, page 108	**Glaze**
Cream Filling, page 109	1¼ cups sifted confectioners' sugar
1¼ cups granulated sugar	2 tablespoons soft butter or margarine
4 orange slices	
2 lemon slices	3 tablespoons milk
¾ cup light rum	¼ teaspoon vanilla extract
⅔ cup apricot preserves	Whipped cream
2 teaspoons lemon juice	Assorted candied fruits

1. Make Spongecake Layers and Cream Filling. Cool.

2. In medium saucepan, combine granulated sugar with 1 cup water; bring to boiling, stirring until sugar is dissolved. Boil, uncovered, 10 minutes.

3. Reduce heat. Add orange and lemon slices; simmer 10 minutes. Discard orange and lemon slices. Add rum.

4. Meanwhile, split each cake layer crosswise, to make 6 layers in all. Spoon rum syrup evenly over all layers.

5. Using about 1¼ cups Cream Filling between each 2 layers, put

round layers together on a large round dish, with the 9-inch layers at bottom.

6. Cut 4 strips 3¼ inches wide from square layers. Cut each strip crosswise into thirds. Spread one side of each piece lightly with remaining Cream Filling.

7. With filling toward cake, place pieces around base of round cake layers, pressing firmly against layers. (If necessary, trim last piece to fit.)

8. Cut a long piece of plastic film, and wrap tightly around side of cake; cover top with another piece. Refrigerate overnight.

9. Next day: Melt apricot preserves in small saucepan; strain. Add lemon juice. Remove film from cake. Brush preserves mixture over entire surface of cake. Refrigerate.

10. Make Glaze: In small bowl, combine confectioners' sugar with butter, milk, and vanilla; beat until smooth.

11. Brush glaze over entire surface of cake. Decorate with whipped cream and candied fruit. Refrigerate until serving.

Makes 16 servings.

Spongecake Layers	½ teaspoon salt
1 cup milk	6 eggs (1⅓ cups)
2 cups sifted all-purpose flour	2 cups sugar
2 teaspoons baking powder	2 teaspoons vanilla extract

1. Heat milk in small saucepan until bubbles form around edge of pan. Remove from heat.

2. Preheat oven to 350°F.

3. Sift flour with baking powder and salt; set aside.

4. In large bowl of electric mixer, at high speed, beat eggs until thick and lemon-colored. Gradually add the sugar, beating until the mixture is smooth and well blended—about 5 minutes.

5. At low speed, beat in flour mixture just until smooth. Add warm milk and vanilla, beating just until combined.

6. Turn batter into an ungreased 9-inch round layer-cake pan, an ungreased 8-inch round layer-cake pan, and an ungreased 8-by-8-by-2-inch baking pan (pour slightly less batter into square pan).

7. Bake 25 to 30 minutes, or until cake tester inserted in center comes out clean. Invert pans by hanging between two other pans. Let cake layers cool completely before removing from pans.

Makes 3 layers.

Cream Filling
1 cup sugar
½ cup cornstarch
1 quart milk
Peel of 1 lemon, in large pieces

4 egg yolks, slightly beaten
½ teaspoon vanilla extract
2 tablespoons finely chopped
  mixed candied fruit
⅓ cup chopped semi-sweet-
  chocolate pieces

1. In medium saucepan, combine sugar and cornstarch. Gradually add milk, stirring constantly. Add lemon peel.

2. Bring to boiling, stirring constantly; boil 1 minute. Stir a little of hot mixture into egg yolks; return to saucepan, stirring. Bring to boiling; then remove from heat. Remove and discard peel. Stir in vanilla.

3. Refrigerate the mixture, covered, until it is well chilled—at least 3 hours.

4. Stir in the candied fruit and chopped chocolate. Refrigerate until ready to use.

Sicilian Cream Cake

CASSATA ALLA SICILIANA

Spongecake, page 110

Rum Syrup
1¼ cups granulated sugar
4 orange slices
2 lemon slices
⅔ cup golden rum

Cheese Filling
1 pound ricotta cheese
½ cup confectioners' sugar
½ cup semi-sweet-chocolate
  pieces, chopped

1 jar (4 ounces) mixed candied
  fruit, finely chopped
1 tablespoon golden rum
2 tablespoons semi-sweet-
  chocolate pieces, melted

⅓ cup seedless raspberry jam
1 cup heavy cream
2 tablespoons confectioners'
  sugar
Candied cherries

1. Make Spongecake.

2. Make Rum Syrup: In small saucepan, combine granulated sugar, 1 cup water, and the orange and lemon slices. Bring to boiling, stirring until sugar is dissolved. Boil gently, uncovered, 20 minutes. Discard fruit slices. Stir in ⅔ cup rum; set aside.

3. Make Cheese Filling: In medium bowl, combine ricotta and ½ cup

confectioners' sugar; beat with electric mixer until well combined—about 3 minutes. Stir in ½ cup chopped chocolate pieces, the chopped mixed candied fruit, and 1 tablespoon rum.

4. For chocolate-cheese filling: Remove 1 cup cheese filling to small bowl, and stir in melted chocolate pieces until well blended. Refrigerate both fillings until ready to assemble cake.

5. To assemble cake: Split each spongecake layer in half, to make 4 layers in all. Place a layer, cut side up, on serving plate. Drizzle with ½ cup of the rum syrup. Then spread with half of the plain cheese filling.

6. Spread cut side of second layer with half of the raspberry jam. Place, jam side down, over cheese layer. Drizzle with ½ cup rum syrup. Spread with all the chocolate-cheese filling.

7. Add third layer, cut side up. Drizzle with ½ cup syrup. Spread with remaining plain cheese filling. Spread remaining jam over cut side of fourth layer. Place, jam side down, over cheese layer. Drizzle on remaining syrup.

8. Beat cream with confectioners' sugar until stiff. Use to frost side and top of cake. If desired, place some of cream in pastry bag with rosette tip, and use to decorate cake. Garnish with candied cherries.

9. Refrigerate at least 4 hours, or until serving time.
Makes 10 servings.

Spongecake for Cassata

7 eggs	1 tablespoon grated lemon peel
1 cup confectioners' sugar	1 tablespoon sweet Vermouth
1 cup sifted cake flour	

1. Separate eggs, placing whites in large bowl, yolks in another large bowl. Set aside until whites warm to room temperature—about 1 hour.

2. Preheat oven to 350°F. Butter two 8-inch round layer-cake pans, and dust with confectioners' sugar.

3. Add 1 cup confectioners' sugar to egg yolks; with electric mixer at high speed, beat until thick and lemon-colored—about 5 minutes. Add flour, lemon peel, and Vermouth; beat at low speed until well combined.

4. Wash and dry beaters. Then beat egg whites until stiff peaks form when beater is slowly raised.

5. Fold one third of the whites into egg-yolk mixture until well combined. Then fold in remaining whites just until combined. Turn into prepared pans.

6. Bake 25 to 30 minutes, or until top springs back when gently pressed

with fingertip. Cool in pans 10 minutes; then remove to rack, and let cool completely.

Makes 2 layers.

Italian Fried Twists

CENCI

4 cups unsifted cake flour	2 tablespoons brandy
¼ cup butter or margarine	Salad oil or shortening for
⅓ cup granulated sugar	deep-frying
4 eggs	Confectioners' sugar

1. Place flour in a large bowl. With pastry blender, cut in the butter until the mixture resembles coarse crumbs. Then stir in the granulated sugar.

2. In small bowl, lightly beat eggs with brandy. Add to flour mixture, stirring until all flour is moistened. On lightly floured surface, knead dough until smooth—about 5 minutes. Cover, and let rest 10 minutes.

3. In deep-fat fryer or heavy saucepan, slowly heat salad oil (4 inches deep) to 400°F. on deep-frying thermometer.

4. Meanwhile, cut off one-sixth of dough at a time, and roll to paper thinness. With pastry cutter or knife, cut into strips 8 inches long and ¾ inch wide; tie some into knots. If desired, cut some of dough into 2-inch diamonds.

5. Gently drop dough shapes, a few at a time, into hot oil, and cook 1 minute, or until very lightly browned. With slotted utensil or tongs, lift out of oil, and drain on paper towels. Let cool.

6. Sprinkle with confectioners' sugar. May be stored, loosely covered, in a dry place.

Makes about 8 dozen.

Macaroons

AMARETTI

2 egg whites	¼ teaspoon salt
1½ cups blanched almonds, ground	1 teaspoon almond extract
1 cup sifted confectioners' sugar	½ teaspoon vanilla extract
	Blanched almonds

1. In large bowl of electric mixer, let egg whites warm to room temperature—about 1 hour.

2. Preheat oven to 300°F. Lightly grease cookie sheets.

3. In medium bowl, combine the ground almonds with the sugar, mixing well.

4. Beat egg whites with salt until stiff peaks form when beaters are slowly raised. Using a wooden spoon, stir almond mixture into the beaten egg whites, along with the almond and vanilla extracts, just until well combined.

5. Drop by slightly rounded teaspoonfuls, 2 inches apart, onto prepared cookie sheets. Top each with a blanched almond.

6. Bake 20 minutes, or until a light-brown color. With spatula, remove to wire rack to cool completely.

7. Store, covered, overnight.

Makes 2½ to 3 dozen.

Anise Toast

PANE ALL'ANICE

2½ cups sifted cake flour	1 cup sugar
2 teaspoons baking powder	3 eggs
¼ teaspoon salt	1 tablespoon anise extract
¼ cup butter or margarine, softened	

1. Preheat oven to 350°F. Grease and flour 2 cookies sheets.

2. Sift flour with baking powder and salt 3 times; set aside.

3. In medium bowl, with portable electric mixer at medium speed, beat butter with sugar until very light. Add eggs, one at a time, beating well after each addition. Beat in anise.

4. Add flour mixture; beat, at low speed, until blended. Divide mixture in half. Spread each half on a cookie sheet to 11-by-5-inch oval.

5. Bake 15 to 20 minutes, or until pale golden brown. Remove from oven; cut into 1-inch-thick slices. Turn each on its side. Bake 10 to 15 minutes, or until lightly browned.

6. Remove slices to wire rack, and let cool completely.

Makes 18 to 20.

Sesame-seed Cookies

REGINA

2 cups unsifted all-purpose flour	⅔ cup shortening
¾ cup sugar	2 egg yolks
1½ teaspoons baking powder	¼ cup milk
¼ teaspoon salt	1 teaspoon vanilla extract
	⅓ cup sesame seeds

1. Preheat oven to 375°F. Grease cookie sheet.

2. Into bowl, sift flour, sugar, baking powder, and salt. With pastry blender, cut in shortening until mixture resembles coarse crumbs.

3. Add egg yolks, milk, and vanilla; with fork, mix just until dough holds together. Knead several times, or until smooth.

4. For each cookie, shape rounded tablespoonful of dough into an oval, to resemble little loaf of bread. Roll in sesame seeds, coating completely. Place on prepared cookie sheet.

5. Bake 15 to 20 minutes, or until brown. Let cool on wire rack. Makes 2½ dozen.

Little Knot Cookies

NODITINI

5½ cups unsifted all-purpose flour	4 eggs
¾ cup butter or margarine	½ cup milk
1½ cups sugar	1 teaspoon lemon extract
1 tablespoon baking powder	1 teaspoon anise extract

1. Place flour in a large bowl. With pastry blender, cut in butter until mixture resembles coarse crumbs. Stir in sugar and baking powder until well combined.

2. In small bowl, lightly beat eggs with milk and extracts. Add to flour mixture, stirring until all flour is moistened. Turn out on well-floured surface, and knead until smooth—about 2 minutes.

3. Refrigerate, covered, 1 hour.

4. Preheat oven to 325°F.

5. Cut off a small piece of dough and roll it, on a lightly floured surface, into a pencil-thin strip 6 inches long. Twist in a loose knot or a braid, and place on ungreased cookie sheet. Repeat until all dough is used.

6. Bake 20 minutes, or until lightly browned. Remove to rack; cool. Makes about 10 dozen.

Pine-nut Cookies

PINOCATTE

½ cup granulated sugar	1 can (8 ounces) almond paste
½ cup confectioners' sugar	2 egg whites, slightly beaten
¼ cup unsifted all-purpose flour	1 jar (3 ounces) Italian pignolias
⅛ teaspoon salt	Confectioners' sugar

1. Preheat oven to 300°F. Lightly grease 2 large cookie sheets. Sift sugars with flour and salt; set aside.

2. In medium bowl, break up almond paste with wooden spoon. Add egg whites, and beat until well blended and fairly smooth. Stir in flour mixture until well blended.

3. Drop mixture by slightly rounded teaspoonfuls, 2 inches apart, on prepared cookie sheets. Lightly press into rounds 1½ inches in diameter. Press some pignolias into each.

4. Bake 20 to 25 minutes, or until golden. Remove to wire rack; cool. Sprinkle with confectioners' sugar.

Makes about 2½ dozen.

Nougat

TORRONE

In Italy pieces of torrone are carefully wrapped in silver paper for Christmas giving.

1 cup blanched filberts	½ cup honey
2 cans (4½-ounce size) blanched whole almonds	¼ teaspoon salt
2 cups sugar	2 egg whites
1 cup light corn syrup	2 teaspoons vanilla extract
	¼ cup soft butter or margarine

1. Preheat oven to 350°F. Spread filberts and almonds on cookie sheet. Toast in oven 10 to 15 minutes—just until golden. Set aside.

2. In heavy, straight-side, 3-quart saucepan, combine sugar, corn syrup, honey, salt, and ¼ cup water. Stir, over medium heat, until sugar is dissolved.

3. Continue cooking to 252°F. on candy thermometer, without stirring, or until a small amount in cold water forms a hard ball.

4. Meanwhile, in large bowl of electric mixer, at high speed, beat egg whites until stiff peaks form when beater is slowly raised.

5. In a thin stream, pour about one fourth of hot syrup over egg whites, beating constantly, at high speed, until mixture is stiff enough to hold its shape—3 to 5 minutes.

6. Continue cooking rest of syrup to 315° to 318°F. on candy thermometer, or until a small amount in cold water forms brittle threads.

7. In a thin stream, pour hot syrup over meringue, beating constantly, at high speed, until mixture is stiff enough to hold its shape.

8. Add vanilla and butter, beating until thickened again—about 5 minutes. With wooden spoon, stir in toasted nuts.

9. Turn mixture into a buttered 11-by-7-by-1¼-inch pan; smooth top with a spatula.

10. Refrigerate until firm.

11. Loosen edge of candy all around; turn out in large block. With sharp knife, cut into 1½-by-1-inch pieces.

12. Wrap each piece individually in waxed paper. Store in refrigerator. Makes about 2½ pounds.

Index